# Wrongful Adoption:
## Law, Policy, & Practice

Madelyn Freundlich & Lisa Peterson

D1559812

CWLA Press
Washington, DC

The Evan B. Donaldson
Adoption Institute
New York, NY

CWLA Press is an imprint of the Child Welfare League of America. The Child Welfare League of America (CWLA) is a privately supported, non-profit, membership-based organization committed to preserving, protecting, and promoting the well-being of all children and their families. Believing that children are our most valuable resource, CWLA, through its membership, advocates for high standards, sound public policies, and quality services for children in need and their families.

CHILD WELFARE LEAGUE OF AMERICA, INC.
440 First Street, NW, Third Floor, Washington, DC 20001-2085
E-mail: books@cwla.org

CURRENT PRINTING (last digit)
10 9 8 7 6 5 4 3 2 1

Cover design by Veronica J. Morrison

Printed in the United States of America

ISBN # 0-87868-737-8

*Library of Congress Cataloging-in-Publication Data*
Freundlich, Madelyn.
    Wrongful adoption  :    law, policy, & practice / Madelyn Freundlich & Lisa Peterson.
       p.   cm.
    Includes bibliographical references.
    ISBN 0-87868-737-8
    1. Adoption--Law and legislation--United States. 2. Disclosure of information--Law and legislation--United States. 3. Adoption agencies--United States.    I. Peterson, Lisa.   II. Title.
    KF545.F74   1998                                              98-27226
    346.7301'78--dc21                                                 CIP

# Contents

# Introduction

Over the last decade, adoption agencies increasingly have confronted issues about obtaining and disclosing information to prospective adoptive families about the health and social background of children and their birth families. Quality practice supports the sharing of such information. Litigation related to this issue has shown, however, that in a number of cases, adoption agencies and independent practitioners have failed to provide prospective adoptive families with known information about a child's physical, emotional, or developmental problems or with critical background information about the child's birth family and history. In these cases, adoptive families, deprived of such information, have found themselves neither emotionally nor financially prepared to care for a child whose needs require enormously expensive medical or mental health treatment. Some of these families have sought redress in the courts.

In response to litigation initiated by adoptive families, courts have recognized a duty to disclose known material information about a child's health and social background to prospective adoptive families. Although the duty to disclose applies to agencies and independent practitioners alike, most of the cases to date have involved agencies. In the face of a breach of the duty to disclose, courts have held agencies liable for the tort of "wrongful adoption" and awarded adoptive families monetary damages. An agency's breach of the duty to disclose can take many forms and, depending on the state, liability may be imposed when agencies misrepresent a child's background, deliberately withhold information, or are negligent in providing prospective adoptive parents with information that could be material to their decision whether to adopt a particular child.

While courts have provided a legal remedy to adoptive families harmed by failures to disclose, state legislatures have focused on preventive action. They have undertaken, through statute, to define the disclosure obligations of adoption practitioners to reduce the incidence of "wrongful adoption" and facilitate informed decision making by adoptive families.

The judicial and statutory developments over the past decade have addressed adoption practitioners' conduct in relation to domestic adoptions. Case law and state statutes have responded to failures to disclose in domestic adoptions handled privately by agencies or independent practitioners and in adoptions of children in foster care in this country. Wrongful adoption suits only recently have been considered in relation to international adoption. This development coincides with the growth in the number of children adopted from other countries and the incidence of serious health, emotional, and developmental problems among children adopted from abroad.

This monograph examines wrongful adoption in four parts. Chapter 1 reviews the historical and social context of adoption practice in relation to disclosure of children's health and other background information to prospective adoptive parents, outlines the benefits of disclosure for all parties to an adoption, and discusses the factors that may be related to failure to disclose. Chapter 2 discusses the cases that have shaped the tort of "wrongful adoption," applies "wrongful adoption" theory to international adoption, and discusses state statutes that set forth disclosure obligations. Chapter 3 discusses some of the key policy and practice issues that warrant close consideration in relation to disclosure of health and other background information. Finally, Chapter 4 provides recommendations to enhance agencies' abilities to implement quality practice in the area of disclosure of health and other background information and limit exposure to liability for wrongful adoption.

# An Overview

## The Historical and Social Context

Policies and practice with regard to the disclosure of medical and social background information to prospective adoptive families have changed over time. Agency approaches have been cyclical, reflecting changes in the social environment and differing definitions of quality adoption practice.

During the first half of the twentieth century, the majority of adoption agencies had full disclosure policies that supported providing adoptive parents with all the facts in a child's case record. It was standard practice for agencies to review the child's history with the adoptive parents, including the child's health status and history, the results of any psychometric testing, and as much as was known about the child's heredity [Carp 1995]. Full disclosure was relatively easy in the early decades of the twentieth century, as adoption records usually did not contain extensive health or social background information, and there was often little family information to share. In the 1930s and up until World War II, the majority of adopted children were older, and they had memories of their parents and backgrounds [Carp 1995]. As a result, the information that social workers conveyed to adoptive families was information that the children already knew about their backgrounds and could themselves share. Social work values in this era also supported full disclosure to adoptive parents. Social work ideals at the time promoted sharing with adult adopted persons and birth families all known family information upon request and, similarly, supported full disclosure of background information to adoptive families [Carp 1995]. Agencies were further influenced by the eugenics movement of the early 1900s and were especially attentive to communicating health or social information to prospective adoptive families if there was any indication that a child's birth parent was "diseased" or "feeble-minded" [Carp 1995, citing Watson 1918: 113].

The adoption standards of the Child Welfare League of America in 1932 reflected the values and practice of the time:

> Children with special handicaps of a physical nature or related to personality or behavior, and those whose heredity suggests that difficult problems may arise, should be placed for adoption only when the adoptive parents thoroughly understand the child's condition and needs [CWLA 1932: 23].

Beginning in the 1950s, however, restrictions began to be placed on the disclosure of health and social history to adoptive parents. Two dynamics were at work: concerns about protecting adopted children from the stigma associated with illegitimacy, and efforts to accommodate what social workers construed as a general reluctance on the part of adoptive families to discuss adoption with their children [Carp 1995]. In the 1950s, the rate of out-of-wedlock births began to increase dramatically, with a concomitant increase in the number of infants who needed adoption services [Carp 1995]. Illegitimacy was viewed as a source of shame for both the birth mother and her child [Gonyo & Watson 1988]. At the same time, adoption itself was viewed with skepticism because it involved bringing children of "different blood" into families [Hollinger 1990; Feigelman & Silverman 1986; Dukette 1984]. Research in the 1940s and 1950s revealed the anxieties of adoptive parents about the fact of adoption. Studies showed that many adoptive parents postponed telling their children they were adopted, and many others deliberately failed to recall any of the background information they were given at time of placement, telling their children that they did not have any information on the children's birth parents [Hutchinson 1943; Lockridge 1947; Raymond 1955]. The 1950s saw the formulation and implementation of policies of greater secrecy to protect birth parents and adoptees from the stigma of illegitimate birth and to shelter adoptive families from public knowledge that they could not have their own biological children and had adopted their children [Daly & Sobol 1997].

The 1950s also ushered in greater reliance on psychoanalytic theory in placing a child. The literature of the decade urged agencies to withhold from prospective adoptive families all information about the child's birth family [Carp 1995]. This absolute ban on sharing information was advocated on the basis of psychoanalytical principles: adoptive parents were theorized as neurotic and envious of those who could bear children, and adopted children were characterized as unable to resolve the Oedipus complex if told that their births were illegitimate [Kohlsaat & Johnson 1954]. Social workers largely rejected recommendations that background information be completely withheld. Support, however, grew for "selective and positive" disclosure of the biological family's background [Carp 1995]. The debate centered on how much family information should be disclosed and how much withheld.

By the mid-1950s, social work practice had become that of giving only "selected background material," with all "sordid or irrelevant" details deleted [Schapiro 1956: 86-87]. Adoption professionals maintained that sharing only favorable information would assist the child in building a sense of positive self-esteem. Irrelevant or unverified information (which included background medical and genetic information) was of little benefit to the parent-child relationship, and such information could cause damage by arousing anxiety and apprehension [Carp 1995]. In particular, the sharing of such information as incest, paternal incarceration, or the "incorrigibility" of the birth mother was considered inappropriate because of the distress that such information could cause adoptive parents [Cady & Cady 1956].

The practice of selective disclosure was consistent with the prevailing view of adoption in the 1950s, which insisted that adoption was "the same" as biological family formation and also maintained that the adopted child was indistinguishable from a child born to the family [Cole & Donley 1990]. The withholding of negative background material served to minimize any differences between the adoptive family and the birth family, thereby preserving the idea that adopting a child was in no way different than having a biological child of one's own [Carp 1995]. Sharing only positive information with adoptive parents also responded to adoptive parents' concerns about sharing too much information with the child about his or her background. Adoptive parents could, "with true peace of mind," legitimately claim ignorance as to any less-than-positive information when asked questions about their children's birth families [Raymond 1955].

The change in practice from full to selective disclosure was reflected in the CWLA revision of its adoption standards in 1959. The standard was rewritten to advise adoption agencies that they should not give to adoptive parents "information which is not relevant to the child's development and would only arouse anxiety" [CWLA 1959:27].

Beginning in the 1970s, social work practice began to shift once again toward greater sharing of information. Three factors largely influenced this change in practice. First, the population of children needing adoption began to shift from healthy, white infants (who had been the children primarily available for adoption) to older children with special needs [Carp 1995]. As changes in sexual mores began to diminish the stigma associated with nonmarital child bearing and single parenthood, the number of infants available for adoption significantly declined [Mosher & Bachrach 1996]. At the same time, child welfare reforms were initiated and the adoption of children in foster care and in institutional settings became a greater policy priority [Cole & Donley 1990]. For these children, who often were older and had special needs, health and family background information was of particular importance, and adoption professionals recognized that such information should be shared with prospective adoptive families [Cole 1990].

Second, adoption professionals began to recognize that, contrary to earlier assumptions, adoptive parents were interested in parenting children with special needs and were not discouraged when they were told difficult background information [Barth & Berry 1988; Groze et al. 1992]. Prospective adoptive parents came forward, not with the expectation of adopting a perfect infant, but open to adopting older children and children with disabilities.

Finally, greater disclosure was prompted by the adoption self-help, support, and advocacy movements of the 1970s that led to greater demands by all members of the adoption triad, but particularly by adult adoptees, for more participation and control over the critical issues that affected them [Cole & Donley 1990]. Birth parents, adopted individu-

als, and adoptive families began to speak openly about the losses related to the adoption experience, the differences between adoption and
biological parenting, and the need for greater sharing of background
information [Wertkin 1986]. The Freedom of Information Act con-
ferred further authority on the demands of all triad members for more
information [Cole & Donley 1990].

In 1978, CWLA again revised its adoption standards in response to
these practice developments. The 1978 standards deleted references to
withholding adverse information and emphasized the importance of
providing adoptive parents with the child's developmental, medical,
and genetic history, as well as nonidentifying information about the
birth family [CWLA 1978: 47-48].

The 1990s ushered in an environment of openness, disclosure of
personal matters, and revelation [Diamond 1997]. The proliferation of
daytime "talk shows" and "tell-all" books demonstrated wide social ac-
ceptance of the sharing of the most intimate details by the famous and
not-famous. The growth of computerized information systems and tech-
nological management of public and private data significantly limited
the extent to which the privacy of information could be assured. As
information became more readily available, it no longer was possible to
control access or guarantee confidentiality [Diamond 1997].

At the same time, biomedical developments in the 1990s emphasized the importance of genetic and biological factors in individuals'
development and health. In the "nature versus nurture" debate, the pen-
dulum swung in favor of "nature": twin studies highlighted the striking
similarities between biologically related individuals, irrespective of radi-
cally different environments [Betsworth et al. 1994; Bouchard & McGue
1990; Rice et al. 1989], and genetic markers increasingly were identified for physical conditions and mental illnesses [Cadoret et al. 1995;
Lombroso et al. 1994]. These findings emphasized the importance of
collecting and communicating health and background information for
children reared outside their biological families.

The CWLA adoption standards, revised in 1988, elaborated further
on the 1978 standards concerning disclosure of background information. The 1988 standards (currently in effect) require the taking of a
developmental history and family history, the completion of a medical

examination, and the use of psychological testing on an as-needed basis. Table 1 outlines the 1988 CWLA standards on the disclosure of nonidentifying information.

## The Benefits of Disclosure and Factors Associated with Failure to Disclose

The importance of disclosing health and other background information is now well recognized by adoption professionals. The benefits of full disclosure flow to children who are placed for adoption, their birth families, prospective adoptive parents, and the adoptive family. For children, disclosure of complete and accurate background information may

- enhance opportunities for early diagnosis and treatment of physical, medical, and psychological problems and conditions;
- promote earlier identification of developmental delays and mobilization of early intervention services to maximize the child's development;
- avoid the need for unnecessary or duplicative testing;
- assist in preventing and/or reducing the risks associated with certain physical or emotional problems;
- provide information that would be important to the adopted adult's own childbearing decisions and information related to the health of his or her descendants; and
- provide critical information to assist the adopted individual, both in childhood and adulthood, in developing a sense of history about himself or herself and a more fully integrated identity [Sullivan 1998; Kopels 1995; Hollinger 1990; Blair 1990].

For birth parents, the agency's collection of health and other background information and disclosure of that information to the child's adoptive parents provide important reassurances. These practices communicate the commitment of the agency to assisting the adoptive family in understanding and meeting the child's needs and to assuring that the child will have important information about his or her origins.

## Table 1. CWLA 1988 Standards on Disclosure of Health and Background Information

| Required Component | Specific Information to Be Obtained |
| --- | --- |
| Developmental History | The following are to be obtained: birth and health history; early development, particularly indications of the way the child "has taken hold of life," such as locomotor development, feeding experiences, and temperament; the child's characteristic way of responding to people and situations; the child's experiences before the adoption decision, particularly maternal attitudes during pregnancy and early infancy, continuity of parental care and affection, foster care placements, and separation experiences; the child's cultural and ethnic background and its impact on values and mores; and language skills, including second language capacities. |
| Family History | A family history is to be obtained from the birth mother and birth father about their family backgrounds and should include any significant hereditary factors or pathology, including illnesses of the birth mother or father that may affect the child's development. |
| Medical Examination | For an infant, the evaluation should include a correlation and interpretation of all available information, including genetic information and laboratory data. For an older child, there should be a complete pediatric examination that includes birth family and developmental history, experiences and adaptations to previous living situations and life experiences, and details about the child's previous medical care. With regard to any existing disability, complete information should be obtained on the type of disability and the treatment and support programs that should be provided to the child and adoptive parents, the extra costs of medical care that can be anticipated, and the plans to subsidize health care if needed. |

For prospective adoptive parents, disclosure of complete and accurate health and other background information about a child facilitates informed decision making. Advising adoptive families of known health and other background information is a critical step toward assuring that families are emotionally and financially prepared to meet a child's special needs. Disclosing such information provides the family with opportunities to seek and obtain adoption subsidies and other resources that the child may need. When families make the decision to adopt based on complete and accurate information, they are far more likely to be prepared to meet the child's current and future needs and to assist the child with identity issues as the child grows and develops. Informed decision making and planning by adoptive families is likely to reduce the possibility of adoption disruption and its consequent trauma on children [Barth & Berry 1988].

Despite the recognized benefits of full and accurate disclosure, recent legal developments illustrate that agencies and independent practitioners have not uniformly disclosed to prospective adoptive parents known health and other background information on children. Although there may be a desire to consider failures to disclose as unusual deviations from standard agency practice, research suggests otherwise. Barth and Berry [1988], in their California-based study of children in foster care who were adopted, found that more than one-third of adoptive families were not told about their adopted child's history of physical abuse and more than one-half who adopted children who were sexually abused were not told of their child's history. They found that, in some cases, social workers appeared not to know the background information, and in others, social workers appeared to be aware of the information but chose not to disclose it. Sachdev [1989], in his broad study of adoptive families, likewise found that adoptive families often do not receive the information about children that they believe they need.

A number of reasons have been advanced to explain agencies' failures to disclose. Listed below are explanations that are frequently given for these failures:

*Fear that children will not be placed if their histories are known leads to hesitancy to disclose information.*

A number of writers have attributed failures to disclose health and other background information to the concerns of adoption caseworkers that such information will lead prospective adoptive families to reject children who are available for adoption [Kopels 1995; Blair 1992; Barth & Berry 1988; Nelson 1985]. Social workers may believe that prospective adoptive families are interested only in healthy children; they may not recognize the benefits for children and adoptive families when background information is fully and accurately shared; or they may fear that if prospective adoptive families were given all the relevant health and other background information, they would decline to adopt the children who need adoptive families. Reports from the field suggest that these dynamics are often at work and that decisions not to share information are guided by fears that prospective adoptive families will be lost as resources.

*Agency staff do not obtain the needed information from birth parents.*

Some writers have focused on deficiencies in gathering health and other background information from birth families that would be critical to full disclosure to prospective adoptive families [Blair 1990]. Practitioners agree that staff may not always obtain all needed information from birth parents. These problems may involve good faith failures to ask certain questions; lack of diligence in asking and following up on questions that could lead to relevant information; and other difficulties, including limited skills in assisting birth families in disclosing sensitive information that they may be reluctant or unwilling to share.

*Agency staff lack access to complete medical histories from sending countries.*

In the context of international adoptions, agencies' failure to disclose health and other background information is often attributed to their inability to obtain full and accurate information from the sending countries. This may be the case notwithstanding an agency's diligent and repeated requests for such information. In addition, the limited information that is received often is not reliable because of the nature of pediatric services available abroad, which often are more limited than in the United States in terms of screening, diagnostic evaluation, and treatment.

### Breakdowns in communication result from understaffing and worker turnover.

In addition to problems associated with obtaining full and accurate information, some writers have pointed to problems in completely and accurately communicating that information [Kopels 1995; Blair 1990]. Some agencies agree with this assessment, pointing to oversized caseloads that limit the time that staff have to devote to each adoptive placement and frequent changes in staff which make it difficult to ensure that the necessary information is communicated.

It is likely that multiple factors are responsible for the failure to fully and accurately disclose known health and other background information to prospective adoptive families and the consequent growth in wrongful adoption lawsuits. Certain factors, in all likelihood, play a critical role—inaccurate assumptions about the interests and information needs of prospective adoptive families, social workers' failure or inability to obtain the needed information from birth families, and inadequate communication procedures within agencies to ensure that information is fully and accurately shared. These factors can be addressed with sound practice and will be discussed more fully in Chapter 4.

# *The Legal Developments*

## The Wrongful Adoption Cases

Wrongful adoption is a cause of action that adoptive parents may assert against adoption agencies or independent practitioners for failure to disclose known health and other background information about the children these parents have adopted. To date, wrongful adoption liability has been based on fraud or negligence.

### Fraud as the Basis for Wrongful Adoption

Wrongful adoption, as a cause of action against adoption agencies, was first recognized on the basis of intentional misconduct that rose to the level of fraud. Although defined slightly differently from state to state, the elements of fraud that generally must be proved are set out in Table 2.

The Ohio Supreme Court issued the first published opinion in the United States imposing liability on an adoption agency for fraudulent misrepresentation. In 1986, in *Burr v. Board of County Commissioners*, the court held that the agency had intentionally misrepresented the child's background to the adoptive parents. The adoptive parents contacted the agency to express an interest in adopting a male child up to 6 months old. The caseworker told the couple about a 17-month-old child whom the agency described as a "nice, healthy baby boy." The caseworker told the couple that the birth mother was 18 years old and single, that the mother had tried to keep the child and work during the day to provide for the child, but that her parents (the child's maternal grandparents), who cared for the child while the mother worked, were "mean" to the child. The agency explained that the birth mother had decided to surrender her child for adoption and leave the state in search of better employment. The couple adopted the child.

**Table 2. Elements of Fraud**

A representation (by the adoption agency);

Which is material to the transaction at hand (the decision to adopt);

Made falsely (by the adoption agency), with knowledge of its falsity or recklessness as to whether it is true or false;

With the intent of misleading another (the adoptive parent) into relying on it;

Justifiable reliance (by the adoptive parent) on the misrepresentation; and

Resulting injury (to the adoptive parent) that was caused by the reliance.

In the ensuing years, the child suffered from a myriad of physical problems. His mental development was classified as delayed. At age 9, he was classified as "educable, mentally retarded" by his school, and he attended special education classes. His condition worsened as he grew older. In high school, he was diagnosed as suffering from Huntington's Disease, a genetic disorder that destroys the central nervous system and is nearly always fatal. During the treatment of the child's disease, the parents obtained a court order to examine the agency's records, and they discovered the statements to them about their child's background were almost entirely false.

The record revealed that the birth mother was a 31-year-old patient in a state mental hospital and that the baby had been born in the facility. The birth father was presumed to be a patient as well. The "mean" grandparents, the birth mother's decision to leave the state in search of better employment, and the voluntary surrender of the child were all fabrications. As far as the child's own background was concerned, the parents learned that prior to placement, the agency had performed a series of psychological assessments on the child that revealed his functioning was below normal. The agency also knew that the child's family background and medical profile put him at risk for developing Huntington's Disease. The only accurate information that the couple received about the child was his age and his gender.

The parents brought suit against the agency, alleging that but for their reliance on the agency's material misrepresentations, they would not have adopted the child. They sought to recover for past medical expenses (which amounted to $81,000 at the time of suit), transportation and lodging costs incurred in consulting medical specialists outside their community, expected funeral expenses, and mental pain and suffering.

In affirming the lower court's finding that the agency had committed fraud, the Ohio Supreme Court wrote in its decision:

> It is not the mere failure to disclose risks inherent in this child's background which we hold to be actionable. Rather, it is the deliberate act of misinforming this couple which deprived them of their right to make a sound parenting decision and which led to the compensable injuries.

The Ohio Supreme Court affirmed the lower court's judgment in favor of the adoptive parents in the amount of $125,000 based on past medical and other expenses and pain and suffering.

Since *Burr*, courts have recognized that fraud can also take the form of deliberate concealment of information in an agency's possession concerning a child's true history as opposed to outright intentional misrepresentations. As with intentional misrepresentation, a case based on allegations of deliberate concealment must establish the elements of fraud. Two landmark deliberate concealment cases are *Michael J. v. Los Angeles County Dept. of Adoptions* [1988] and *Juman v. Louise Wise Services* [1997].

In *Michael J.*, a single woman contacted the agency about a child she had seen on a television program. The program was part of an effort to recruit adoptive parents for the child, who had a highly visible port-wine stain on his upper torso and face. When she first contacted the agency, the woman asked about the stain and was told by the caseworker that it was a birthmark. According to the agency, the child was "suitable for adoption, being in good health, except for the port-wine stain."

The woman adopted the child who, several years after the adoption, began to suffer from seizures. The "birthmark" was discovered to be a manifestation of Sturge-Weber Syndrome, a congenital, degenerative nerve disorder. The adoptive mother sued the agency for wrongful adoption and sought damages for the child's medical expenses and her own emotional distress.

The agency's records, which revealed that the child had been examined prior to placement, contained a description of the port-wine stain and, significantly, a note that "the doctor will not make a definitive statement as to the prognosis for this child." The adoptive mother was never advised as to the doctor's unwillingness to offer a definitive opinion about the child's future health.

The California Court of Appeals held that the adoptive parent could sue for wrongful adoption based on the deliberate concealment of material facts regarding the child's health and remanded the case to the trial court for further proceedings. In the words of the court:

> We are not imposing on the agency a duty to predict the future health of a prospective adoptee. However, there must be a good faith full disclosure of material facts concerning existing or past conditions of the child's health. If the adoptive parent had been informed of the doctor's refusal to make a prognosis, [she] would have been placed on notice, allowing a consideration of the significance of such a refusal and an independent inquiry into the matter.

A few years later, in *Juman v. Louise Wise Services*, New York also recognized a cause of action for deliberate concealment. In *Juman*, the adoptive couple, Martin and Phyllis Juman, applied in 1964 to adopt a healthy infant from a private New York City agency. The agency told the prospective adoptive parents about a 16-month-old boy, relating that the child's birth mother was in her 30s, had won a scholarship to a well-known college, and had completed two years of college course work. The agency told the couple that the birth mother had experienced "some emotional difficulty" after her boyfriend died of a heart attack and, in the midst of her grief, she had become pregnant. The relationship with the birth father was described as "not one of lasting quality." The Jumans proceeded to adopt the child, named Michael.

Beginning at the age of 16 or 17, Michael began to suffer from a number of psychological disorders, requiring multiple hospitalizations.

He was diagnosed as having various forms of mental illness, including depression, bipolar disorder, and schizophrenia. In the course of treating Michael for depression in 1985, his therapist asked the Jumans to obtain information about Michael's birth parents to aid in Michael's treatment. Mr. Juman requested the agency to release any medical and health information it had about Michael. The agency replied with a letter revealing that "the birth mother had a history of episodic depressions for which she was treated psychiatrically. She became involved with the birth father impulsively after the sudden death of her fiancee. We have very little information about the birth father or his family." The letter ended with a statement that "in 1965 [the agency] would have had much less concern about the possible organic nature of depression than [it] would have today."

In 1990, Michael initiated his own efforts to uncover more in-depth information about his birth family and located a member of his birth mother's family. The relative disclosed that Michael's birth mother had a long history of mental illness, had ultimately been diagnosed as schizophrenic, and had undergone a prefrontal lobotomy long before giving birth to him. His birth father had been a mental patient in the hospital where his birth mother had been treated.

Together, Michael and his adoptive parents sued the agency for deliberately concealing the birth parents' true situation, which they alleged was known by the agency prior to placement. The family sought to recover money damages for Michael's medical, hospital, pharmaceutical, and counseling expenses, an amount approaching $2 million. The appellate division of the New York Supreme Court recognized, for the first time in the State of New York, a cause of action for deliberate concealment and referred the case to trial. The Jumans moved at trial for summary judgment on the issue of liability, claiming that the evidence was undisputed that the agency had engaged in fraudulent conduct. The court agreed that the agency had concealed the birth parents' psychiatric histories and had failed to remedy its past silence when given the opportunity to do so in 1985. The court, however, denied the Jumans' motion for summary judgment, holding that there were factual questions to be resolved about the Jumans' reliance on the agency's representations, an essential element of a cause of action for fraud. The case, as of early 1998, awaits further proceedings. Michael Juman committed suicide at age 29 while the case was pending.

## Negligence as a Basis for Wrongful Adoption

After courts recognized a wrongful adoption cause of action based on fraud as illustrated in the *Burr, Michael J.,* and *Juman* cases, they became increasingly willing to impose liability on adoption agencies for negligent conduct that was either clearly unintentional or possibly intentional but where intent was difficult to prove. Courts recognized that an agency's conduct may be just as harmful whether the agency is merely careless in its communications to the adoptive parents (that is, negligent) or purposefully deceptive. The elements of negligence as a basis for a wrongful adoption action that must be proved are generally the same from state to state and are set out in Table 3.

In the early negligence cases, courts imposed a duty on agencies to tell the truth if asked about a child's background by prospective adoptive parents or, if not asked, then only if the agency elected to volunteer background information. Under these rulings, agencies could avoid liability for negligence by refraining from making any representations at all about a child's health history and other background. In the more recent negligence cases, however, courts have held that adoption agencies have an affirmative duty to disclose fully and accurately to adoptive parents all relevant background information in the agencies' possession.

The scope of liability for negligence has evolved similarly to the scope of liability for fraud. Courts first recognized a cause of action for negligent misrepresentation, then for negligent nondisclosure.

The Wisconsin Supreme Court, in *Meracle v. Children's Service Society*, [1989] became the first court in the United States to recognize, in a published opinion, a cause of action against adoption agencies for wrongful adoption based on their negligent misrepresentations about a child's health. In *Meracle*, a couple contacted the agency seeking a "normal, healthy" child. They specifically requested a child without a disabling condition or terminal disease, who was not deformed, and who was of average or above average intelligence. The agency told the adop-

> ## Table 3. Elements of Negligence
> Duty owed by one party (the adoption agency) to another (the prospective adoptive parents);
> Breach of that duty (by the adoption agency); and
> Injury (to adoptive parents) that results from the (agency's) breach of duty.

tive couple about a child whose grandmother had died from Huntington's Disease. The agency advised the parents that the child had no more chance of developing the disease than did any other child because, according to the agency, the disease was transmitted between successive generations and the birth father had tested negative.

Several months after the adoption, the parents learned from a television program that no reliable test had, in fact, yet been developed for determining whether an individual had inherited Huntington's Disease. Subsequently, the child was diagnosed as having the disease. The adoptive parents sued the agency for $10 million in damages for loss of society and companionship of the child, emotional pain and suffering, lost wages, and medical expenses.

The parents never disputed that the agency had accurately revealed to them that Huntington's Disease existed in the child's family background. Instead, they asserted that the misrepresentation occurred when the agency stated incorrectly that the child was not at increased risk of developing the disease. The court held that once an agency voluntarily undertakes to supply health-related information, a duty to use due care arises. In the case under consideration, the court ruled that because the agency had assumed the duty of informing the Meracles about the child's risk of developing Huntington's Disease, it had a duty to accurately represent that information. Although the court held in favor of the adoptive parents, it was quick to add that adoption agencies are under no affirmative duty to disclose health-related information. As the first in a long line of negligence decisions, the *Meracle* holding was quite narrow: to avoid liability, agencies "simply must refrain from making affirmative misrepresentations about a child's health."

The Rhode Island Supreme Court subsequently followed the reasoning of *Meracle* in *Mallette v. Children's Friend and Service* [1995]. In recognizing a cause of action for wrongful adoption based on negligent misrepresentation and applying it specifically to the adoption of children with special health care needs, the court wrote:

> We note that the need for accurate disclosure becomes more acute when special needs children are involved. Parents need to be financially and emotionally equipped to provide an atmosphere that is optimally conducive to that special child's growth and development. Although biological parents can assess the risks of having a child by investigating their own genetic backgrounds, adopting parents remain at the mercy of adoption agencies for information. ... We believe extending the tort of negligent misrepresentation to the adoption context will help alleviate some of the artificial uncertainty imposed on a situation inherent with uncertainty.

In *Mallette*, the family had adopted a seemingly healthy child who was subsequently diagnosed as mentally retarded and severely disturbed. The agency had advised the adoptive parents that the birth mother suffered from learning disabilities that, according to the agency, were caused solely by head trauma the birth mother had experienced as a young child. The adoptive parents asserted that later they learned that the birth mother, in addition to having a myriad of health problems, had been diagnosed as mildly to moderately retarded and that there was only a "possibility" that the retardation was the result of early head trauma. The court held that the agency had negligently misrepresented mental retardation as a learning disability and had negligently attributed the cause to trauma. The court, like the *Meracle* court, imposed liability based on the agency's having volunteered inaccurate background information, noting that agencies could avoid liability by refraining from making any representations at all.

The seminal case for negligent nondisclosure is *M.H. & J.L.H. v. Caritas Family Services* [1992]. In that case, prospective adoptive parents applied to the agency to adopt a baby. The agency contacted the prospective adoptive parents and asked whether they would consider adopting a child with incest in the child's background. According to the home study summary, the couple "appeared open to any child except one with a very serious mental deficiency." The agency subsequently informed them about a child for whom there was a "possibility of incest in the family." The agency told the couple that there was a slight chance that the child might have abnormalities related to incest in his "background." The couple adopted the child based on their understanding that incest in the child's background would not affect the child's health.

From an early age, the child experienced serious behavioral and emotional problems. One of the child's psychologists contacted the adoption agency for more information on the child's background. The agency responded with a document that, for the first time, revealed that the child's parents were a 17-year-old boy and his 13-year-old sister. The agency then admitted that it knew of this relationship when it first considered placing the child for adoption.

The adoptive parents filed suit, alleging that the agency failed to disclose the relationship of the child's birth parents and all relevant history that it had about the birth parents. The adoptive parents never disputed that the agency had told them that there was a "possibility of incest in the adoptee's background." The focus of their complaint was that the agency had failed to inform them that the child's birth parents were siblings. The adoptive parents sought recovery for their mental pain and suffering as well as for the child's considerable mental health treatment expenses.

In recognizing a cause of action based on negligent nondisclosure, the court found a "legal duty to not mislead ... by only partially disclosing the truth." As in *Meracle* and *Mallette*, the court declined to impose an affirmative duty on agencies to disclose all known facts about a child's health and genetic background. The court was only willing to mandate that once an agency undertakes disclosure of information, it must do so completely and accurately. With regard to damages, the court held that the adoptive parents could recover for loss of services, advice, comfort, and protection resulting from their child's severe problems, but the court denied recovery for emotional distress or for punitive damages, finding insufficient evidence to support these claims.

## Imposition of an Affirmative Duty to Disclose

The tide began to shift in favor of recognizing an affirmative duty to disclose in *Roe v. Catholic Charities of the Diocese of Springfield* [1992]. In this Illinois appellate court case, the court refused to accord the agency the discretion to decide if and when it would disclose background information to prospective adoptive parents. The court held that an agency has a duty to answer honestly and completely all questions posed by prospective adoptive parents concerning children's background. The court concluded that "since [the] adoption agency is the only one of these parties with the information concerning the infants' physical and psychological health, the burden can be placed on no other party."

In *Roe*, three different couples approached the agency, each seeking to adopt a "normal" and "healthy" child. The agency placed a child in each family's home as a foster child with the potential for future adoption. Each set of prospective adoptive parents stipulated to the agency that they would adopt a child only if all the child needed was "lots of love," the child was physically and mentally "normal," the agency would tell them all they knew about the child's background, and they would incur no unusual or extraordinary medical expense for the child's care. The agency indicated that each child placed with the families met these criteria. With regard to each couple's requirement that the agency disclose all known background information, the agency stated that it had no information concerning the children's backgrounds.

Each couple adopted the child who had been placed in their home. Each child subsequently displayed aggressive and destructive behavior, and one of the three children later required institutionalization. In each case, the adoptive parents incurred extraordinary medical expenses that were expected to continue to mount. Each couple obtained a court order to review the agency's records, whereupon they learned for the first time their child's true history. The couples sued the agency for nondisclosure.

The records revealed that, although the agency had represented to the families that the children were normal and healthy and claimed that it had no background information, the agency actually knew that each of these children had serious behavioral problems. These problems ranged from one child smearing feces on the walls of a former foster home to another child stomping to death the dog of a former foster family. All of the children had seen psychiatrists, psychologists, and/or other mental health professionals for their destructive and violent behavior, and two of the three children had been diagnosed as emotionally and socially disturbed.

In light of the adoptive families' forthright approach with the agency (as evidenced by their clear descriptions of the type of child each sought to adopt) and their requests for all known information concerning the children, it was not difficult for the court to impose a duty on the agency to answer questions truthfully. The court made clear that an agency has a duty to give full information once it volunteers any information, whether or not prospective adoptive parents specifically request the additional information. The *Roe* court, however, stopped short of imposing a general duty to affirmatively disclose all information known to an agency.

Then came *Gibbs v. Ernst* [1994], in which the Pennsylvania Supreme Court charted new territory. The *Gibbs* court held that " an adoption agency has a duty to disclose fully and accurately to the adopting parents all relevant nonidentifying information in its possession concerning the adoptee," reasoning that "the unique relationship between the adoption agency and the adoptive parents gives rise to such a responsibility." The *Gibbs* court made clear that an agency could no longer avoid liability simply by refraining from making any disclosure.

In *Gibbs*, the prospective adoptive parents inquired about the availability of a healthy, white infant for adoption. In view of the long waiting list, the agency encouraged the couple to consider a "hard-to-place due to age" child and stated that it would disclose any physical or sexual abuse in the child's history. The prospective adoptive parents subsequently requested that a child considered "hard-to-place due to age" be placed with them, but specified that they did not wish to adopt a child with a history of sexual or physical abuse or with any mental or emotional problems. The agency told the couple about a 5-year-old boy who had been placed in foster care because of neglect and whose stay in care for two years had been with only one family. The agency indicated that the child was hyperactive but specifically denied that he had been a victim of any physical or sexual abuse. Prior to finalization of the adoption, the couple asked the agency whether there was any information in the files concerning the child that had not been disclosed to them. The agency assured the couple that all information in the agency's possession had been communicated.

After the adoption was finalized, the child became violent and aggressive toward other children and required inpatient psychiatric care. He was diagnosed as schizophrenic and given a guarded prognosis. During one of the child's many hospitalizations, the adoptive family learned for the first time that the agency had known, but never disclosed to them, that the child had a long history of physical and sexual abuse, a number of foster care placements before being freed for adoption, and a history of aggression toward other children.

The *Gibbs* court held that the agency had an affirmative duty to disclose all relevant nonidentifying information in its possession. The court stated that "the only burden on adoption intermediaries is the obligation to make a reasonable investigation of their records, and to make reasonable efforts to reveal fully and accurately all nonidentifying information in their possession to the adopting parents." The court, however, declined to impose a duty to uncover health and other background information that was not provided to the agency, requiring at most a "good faith effort to obtain a child's medical history" and, if unobtainable, to state the reason for its omission.

In *Mohr v. Commonwealth* [1995], the Massachusetts Supreme Court followed the lead of the *Gibbs* court in holding that an adoption agency "does have an affirmative duty to disclose to adoptive parents information about a child that will enable them to make a knowledgeable decision about whether to accept the child for adoption." In this case, the prospective adoptive parents approached the agency and stated that, while they could accept a child with a "correctable medical problem" or an emotional problem, they did not feel they could consider a "special needs" child. The agency then told the adoptive parents about a 6-year-old girl who had been placed in foster care at birth. The agency explained that the birth mother was young and wanted to go into nursing, and reported there was no background information on the birth father. The agency further stated that although there were no medical records available concerning the child, it was known that the child had been removed and placed in foster care because of abuse, had been hospitalized previously for malnutrition, was small for her age, and had been examined for dwarfism. In the petition that the agency prepared for the court that finalized the adoption, the agency wrote that the child "was developing below average due to environmental deprivation, but had potential for further development." The birth mother was described as "generally in good health."

After the adoption, the child showed persistent signs of stunted growth and behavioral disruption, prompting further evaluations and a request from the child's pediatrician for a complete medical history. Some 10 years later, the parents discovered that the records obtained by the pediatrician contained information showing that the agency had known but intentionally withheld from the parents significant facts, including that the birth mother was schizophrenic and a patient in the state mental hospital and that the child had been diagnosed as mentally retarded with cerebral atrophy.

The parents sued to recover damages sufficient to enable them to provide their daughter with the residential care that she would need throughout her life. By the time of trial, the adoptee, then an adult, had been in and out of institutions and had been diagnosed as schizophrenic. The court held that the agency had an affirmative duty to disclose the birth parents' and the child's background information. As did the *Gibbs* court, the *Mohr* court made clear that it was not addressing whether and to what extent an agency may have a duty to investigate a child's background as opposed to merely reporting what it knows. On the subject of damages, the trial court jury awarded the parents $3.8 million, but this amount was subsequently reduced to the state statutory maximum of $200,000.

In summary, wrongful adoption liability has been based on fraud and negligence, encompassing deliberate misconduct and activity undertaken without due care. Wrongful adoption liability extends both to acts of commission and omission. Figure 1 illustrates the four areas on which wrongful adoption liability may be based.

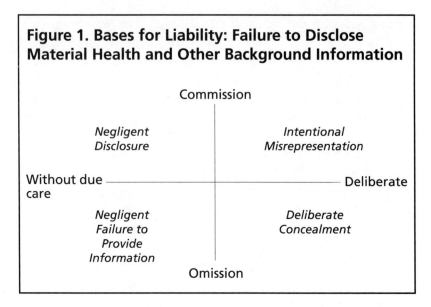

**Figure 1. Bases for Liability: Failure to Disclose Material Health and Other Background Information**

Commission

Negligent Disclosure

Intentional Misrepresentation

Without due care — Deliberate

Negligent Failure to Provide Information

Deliberate Concealment

Omission

## The Remedies for Wrongful Adoption

As the wrongful adoption cases illustrate, adoptive parents generally seek monetary damages to compensate them for the harm they experienced as a result of the agency's fraudulent or negligent conduct. An alternative potential remedy for wrongful adoption is the "annulment" of the adoption, in which adoptive parents seek to set aside an adoption and return the child to the adoption agency [Kopels 1995]. Generally, however, adoptive parents are not seeking to terminate the parent-child relationship and as a result, annulment is a rarely pursued remedy [LeMay 1989].

As the cases reveal, adoptive parents seek money awards for a variety of damages. The type of damages that may be recovered will depend on the theory used—fraud or negligence—and on the scope of damages permitted under the state's laws. The types of damages sought in wrongful adoption cases may include the following:

- **Extraordinary medical expenses.** Adoptive parents may seek and recover medical expenses that have already been incurred and medical expenses that will be incurred in the future, such as lifetime supervised care for a child with a chronic and debilitating medical or mental health condition. Courts differ in the type of extraordinary medical expenses that may be recovered. The *Burr* court, for example, permitted recovery of past expenses only; the *Meracle* court permitted recovery of past and future medical expenses.

- **Costs associated with medical care.** Adoptive parents may seek the incidental expenses associated with obtaining needed medical care, such as transportation and lodging, and the costs of special equipment.

- **Tutoring and other special education expenses** incurred by the family.

- **Lost wages** when adoptive parents must provide the extra care that a child needs.

- **Damages for emotional distress.** Depending on the jurisdiction, adoptive parents may be able to recover for the emotional distress that they or the siblings of the adopted child have experienced. Some jurisdictions, as illustrated by *Meracle*, allow recovery for emotional pain and suffering only when emotional distress manifests itself in the form of physical problems.

- **Damages for physical injury** if the adopted child harms an adoptive parent or a sibling.

- **Punitive damages.** In some jurisdictions, adoptive parents may be able to recover punitive damages if there is fraud or aggravating circumstances are proved and the court determines that additional damages, for the purposes of punishing the agency, are warranted.

Whether adoptive parents should be able to recover the ordinary costs of rearing a child has been hotly debated. On the one hand, some argue that if adoptive parents can establish that they would not have adopted the child had they known of the child's or birth parent's problems, they should be able to recover all of the costs of rearing the child—both the normal and extraordinary expenses [Maley 1987]. On the other hand, the argument is made (and courts that have considered the issue have agreed) that the ordinary costs of rearing a child should not be subject to recovery. This line of reasoning emphasizes that parents who adopt enter into the relationship fully expecting to incur the normal costs of rearing a child. The prevailing view is that, because wrongful adoption is based on the denial of an opportunity to make a fully informed decision about a particular child, the harm that results should be limited to the extraordinary expenses associated with the child's problem or illness

## Wrongful Adoption: Application to International Adoption

Agencies are responsible for collecting health and other background information about children and their birth families and disclosing that information to prospective adoptive families whether an adoption is domestic or international. The scope of wrongful adoption liability, however, has been defined to date primarily in the context of domestic adoptions, and the principles underlying wrongful adoption have only recently begun to be applied by the courts to international adoptions. The extension of wrongful adoption litigation into the arena of international adoptions is an inevitable result of the growth in international adoption over the last decade and the attention that has been given to issues regarding the health and developmental status of children adopted from abroad. Increasingly, international adoptions are of older children who have spent their childhoods in orphanages, an experience that may have profound health and developmental consequences [Barnett & Miller 1996]. At the same time, there have been press accounts of high profile cases in which adoptive parents have been accused of abusing or killing the troubled children they adopted from Eastern Europe and Russia [Engeler 1997; Seelye 1997]—stories that have emphasized the problems that internationally adopted children may have.

Unlike the longer line of domestic wrongful adoption cases, the few decisions in international wrongful adoption cases reported thus far do not reflect a clear path of legal development. One of the commonalities of these cases, however, has been that domestic agencies that facilitate international adoptions may avoid wrongful adoption liability by clearly communicating in writing to prospective adoptive parents the limitations on available information. These cases, it should be noted, solely have addressed the potential liability of agencies in the United States and do not set forth the responsibilities of agencies located in other countries that act as intermediaries for adoption agencies in this country.

In *Harper and Johnson v. Adoption Center of Washington* [1995], the Superior Court of the District of Columbia found in favor of the domestic agency largely because, before the child's placement, the adoptive parents had received complete information in writing about the child's medical condition. The court ruled in favor of the agency even though the adoptive father received the complete medical information on the child only after he arrived in Russia and the information was communicated by the orphanage in a document that was never officially translated.

In *Harper and Johnson*, the adoptive parents sued the agency for allegedly failing to advise them fully, before the adoption, of the fact that the child they adopted had Fetal Alcohol Syndrome (FAS). The court first considered the parents' claims of intentional misrepresentation and fraudulent concealment and concluded that the evidence did not support a claim of fraud. The evidence showed that the agency was unaware of the child's FAS prior to placement and had disclosed in writing all information that it did know, including that the child had a congenital heart defect, before the adoptive parent departed for Russia. The undisputed evidence also showed that the information concerning the child's FAS was only first disclosed by orphanage officials upon the adoptive father's arrival in Russia. In light of this disclosure by Russian officials, the court held that, even if the agency had identified the heart defect as the only known medical problem, it would not have been reasonable for the adoptive parents to have relied on that report as the definitive statement of the child's health status.

The evidence also was undisputed that the adoptive father, Mr. Johnson, had signed a statement in Russia, written in Russian, acknowledging his understanding that, in addition to the child's heart pathology, the child was delayed in her physical, neurological, and psychological development and the delay could be the result of possible FAS. Mr. Johnson sought to have the court set aside the written acknowledgment because the text was in Russian and not officially translated for him, although he admitted that he had signed the document without asking for a complete translation. He explained that he had relied on the explanation of a teenage girl, who was present to translate, that the form simply acknowledged that he had been told of the child's medical history. The court refused to set aside the document, and, instead, held Mr. Johnson accountable for having "made no inquiry in Russia prior to accepting the child as to details of her medical history although he could have done so." In finding for the agency, the court reasoned:

> [The agency] cannot be held responsible for Mr. Johnson's failure to read the documents he was given prior to placement. No agent of the defendant prevented Mr. Johnson from having the documents translated word for word or from making thorough inquiries of the Russian who had first hand knowledge of the child's condition. No reasonable juror could find that Mr. Johnson's exclusive reliance on prior representations sent to the United States was justifiable in light of the complete information readily available to him in Russia.

The agency also was successful in obtaining the dismissal of the adoptive parents' claims of negligent misrepresentation. In the District of Columbia, a plaintiff may not recover on a theory of negligence if the plaintiff's own negligence was a contributing cause of the injury. The court found that Mr. Johnson was himself negligent in two ways. First, he had visited the orphanage repeatedly, had had opportunities to ask questions concerning the child's medical history, but had failed to do so. Second, he failed to examine the relevant records and forms prior to adopting the child and failed to demand a detailed and professional translation of all available documents.

Finally, the court dispensed with the adoptive couple's claim that the agency breached its contract with them. The adoptive parents asserted that they had told the agency that they did not want a child with an uncorrectable medical problem, and the agency violated the contract by placing with them a child with uncorrectable FAS. The court found that the only contract between the parties was a written contract that did not include a promise by the agency to place a child with only correctable conditions. The court noted that the adoptive parents, by their signature, had acknowledged that "it is very difficult to know all the health issues involved" and that the agency could not "guarantee the health of a child, but [would] make best efforts to ensure that the child's health is known to the parent(s) prior to placement."

The court's analysis placed emphasis on the adoptive parents' access to complete medical information in writing prior to placement. The court did not focus on the source of the information (the domestic or international agency), where the information became available (the United States or the other country), or the length of time prior to placement that the adoptive parents acquired the information. The thrust of the court's analysis was not whether the adoptive parents clearly understood the information but whether they had access to a complete medical history in writing and the opportunity to assess its significance. Interestingly, the court did not accord significance to the circumstances in which the adoptive parents found themselves: in a foreign country for the sole purpose of adopting a child, unable to speak the language, and possibly having limited abilities and emotional wherewithal to compare information received prior to departure with that received abroad in order to identify discrepancies and to press for clarification.

Written contracts "rife with cautionary language" insulated another agency from liability in a subsequent international adoption case before the U.S. District Court for the District of Columbia, *Ferenc v. World Child* [1997]. The *Ferenc* court initially considered the adoptive parents' claim on grounds of negligence, but then concluded that the domestic agency's duty to investigate and inform prospective adoptive parents about a child's background was based on a contractual relationship between the prospective parents and the agency. The court found that by the terms of its contract with the adoptive parents, the agency had limited responsibilities with regard to the collection and disclosure of health and other background information.

In *Ferenc*, the adoptive parents of a 3-year-old Russian boy sued the agency for intentionally and/or negligently misrepresenting the true extent of his medical problems. The agency provided the couple with photographs and a three-page English translation of an abstract that described the medical history of the boy, Alexander, that had been prepared by the Russian physician in charge of the orphanage. Among other matters, the abstract disclosed that Alexander had been born prematurely, weighing 4.73 pounds, and that at 3 years of age, he weighed just under 25 pounds and had a head circumference of 18.2 inches. He was said to have "convergent strabismus" and flat feet. A neuropsychiatric entry stated the child's diagnosis was "delay of mental development" which the doctor attributed to "social neglect in the family."

When queried by the couple, the domestic agency stated that the conditions reported appeared to be neither unusual in adopted children from Russia nor uncorrectable. The couple then consulted a general practitioner to whom they showed both the photograph of Alexander and the medical abstract. He refused to offer any opinion on the child's condition and suggested that they request further information. The agency informed the couple that it had access to no information other than that supplied by the orphanage.

The couple traveled to Russia to adopt the child. On arrival, they observed Alexander and spoke with the chief physician who had prepared the abstract. The physician told them that Alexander's strabismus was surgically correctable, the peculiarities they observed in his posture and gait were due to "nutritional deficiencies," and there were no other identified medical problems. The couple was reminded of their right to decline to go forward with the adoption, but they indicated that they wished to proceed. Prior to departing from Russia, the couple, based on their understanding of U.S. immigration requirements, had Alexander examined by Russian physicians at a Moscow clinic who pronounced him "generally healthy." While awaiting their flight home, the couple was told by a Russian staff person, whose source of information was not given, that the child's mother had died of intoxication. After Alexander's arrival in the United States, he was found to be microcephalic, with attention deficit hyperactivity disorder, exhibiting possible symptoms of FAS, and having inoperable strabismus.

The court focused on the adoptive parents' contract with the agency and ruled in the favor of the agency based on an express waiver of "any and all claims" that might arise in favor of the adoptive parents from their relationship with the agency. The waiver, according to the court, "clearly served notice" to the adoptive couple that the agency "did not warrant the success of their efforts, and did not expect to be liable, in whatever respect they might fail or the reasons for its failure, for a less than wholly satisfactory adoption."

Moreover, the court placed great emphasis on the cautionary language that appeared throughout the contract. The document repeatedly referred to the "risk" of intercountry adoptions; it contained a statement to the effect that the agency would furnish medical and social information when it was available, but that it could not guarantee its completeness or accuracy; and it included an acknowledgment by the couple that their child could possibly arrive "with undiagnosed physical, emotional, and/or developmental problems." In several places, the document stated that the adoptive parents were not obliged to accept a child they believed was not healthy. The court also found persuasive that, with respect to Russian children in particular, the document contained nearly two pages of text advising of "ambiguous clinical diagnoses" by Russian physicians and the "problematic state" of Russian medical education and proficiency.

Finally, the court noted that the evidence demonstrated that the adoptive parents understood that they were required to use diligence in making a decision whether to adopt. The court pointed to their consultation with a general practitioner in the United States, their personal observations of Alexander, their questioning of the Russian physician in charge of the orphanage, and their consultation with additional doctors in Moscow immediately prior to their return to the United States. This aspect of the court's decision is somewhat puzzling as it seems to suggest that the more diligence adoptive parents undertake in anticipation of the adoption of a child, the less recourse may later be available to them.

In contrast to *Ferenc*, a recent Wisconsin case suggests that clear written contractual agreements alone may not be enough to insulate adoption agencies from liability for wrongful adoption and that an agency's oral representations will also be considered in assessing liability. In *Nierengarten v. Lutheran Social Services of Wisconsin* [1997], the Wisconsin Court of Appeals raised a cautionary flag regarding agency practices that attempt to interpret the "normalcy" of an adopted child's postplacement "adjustment behavior."

In *Nierengarten,* an adoptive couple contacted an agency in the United States in an effort to adopt a Korean child from an orphanage. The couple received an initial social history, a health history and examination results, and a preflight report from the Korean agency, which stated that the child slept from 8 P.M. to 7 A.M. with a nap, easily adjusted to new circumstances, was even tempered, had good relationships with other children, and was toilet trained. Once in their home, however, the child had extreme tantrums lasting for hours, was in constant motion, slept only five hours per night, was not toilet trained, reacted negatively to new places and people, bit his siblings when he did not get his way, and refused to cooperate with family schedules. On several occasions, the couple spoke with and wrote to agency representatives about the child's conduct and were repeatedly told that the child's behavior was part of a normal adjustment process and would subside. Based on the agency's assurances, the couple finalized the adoption. The child's behavior, however, did not improve, and to attempt to control him, the family installed motion detectors in the house; kept knives, tools, money, and other items locked away; and closely supervised his behavior with their other three children. The child was ultimately hospitalized after a suicide threat and diagnosed with bipolar disorder, attention deficit hyperactivity disorder, and posttraumatic stress disorder.

After the trial court dismissed their complaint for negligent misrepresentation and negligent adoptive placement of the child with their family, the Nierengartens appealed. The Court of Appeals concluded that the trial court was incorrect in dismissing the case, and held that the proceedings should go forward. In remanding the case, the court distinguished between the agency's postplacement and preplacement conduct. The court held that the agency's affirmative oral representations postplacement could form the basis of a claim for negligent misrepresentation, if the agency's conduct occurred after it had obtained additional information indicating that the child suffered from bipolar disorder and other conditions.

The court, however, held that the record did not support a finding of agency negligence prior to placement. The court noted that the agency had not made any representations about the child's health before placement but had, instead, merely transmitted information received from Korea without guaranteeing its accuracy. The couple's Adoption Agreement also indicated that no representation of accuracy had been made. The agreement stated that the agency would "make every effort to ensure that [the] child is healthy and that [the adoptive parents] have as much information about his/her health/family history as possible. [The adoptive parents] understand, however, that [the agency] does not guarantee the information provided [by the Korean agency] will be absolutely accurate."

The court also dismissed the claim for negligent placement based on a duty to investigate. The adoptive family, pointing to the contract language, argued that the agency's agreement to make every effort to provide "as much health/family history information as possible" was breached. They contended that although the agency had provided the preflight report, a health history and physical examination, and initial social history, it did not provide them with certain notes from orphanage records prior to the child's placement with them. In rejecting this argument, the court held that agencies do not a have a common law or statutory duty to provide comprehensive investigations of a child's mental and physical health.

*Nierengarten* suggests that, although agencies may limit their preplacement exposure to liability through carefully written documents, they need to be attentive to any postplacement oral representations they make that adoptive parents may rely on in making the decision to finalize an adoption. Whether in the international adoption context, where courts have generally refused to find preplacement liability, or in domestic adoptions, where preplacement liability has been more readily found, postplacement conduct is an important area of focus in relation to wrongful adoption claims.

## State Disclosure Statutes

Many of the wrongful adoption suits to date involve adoptions that occurred prior to the enactment of state disclosure statutes. Since 1980, most states have enacted statutes mandating that some health information be provided to prospective adoptive families. There is considerable variability in the requirements under state statutes for the collection and disclosure of nonidentifying health and background information. State statutes tend to be somewhat cursory in content, although some states have enacted comprehensive legislation in this area. The key areas in which state statutes on disclosure vary include the following:

- The type of information to be disclosed: medical, health, genetic, social, and educational information;

- The persons as to whom information should be collected: the child, the birth parents, and/or other biological relatives;

- The timing of the disclosure of the information to adoptive parents: whether the information is to be provided prior to placement, prior to finalization, or at finalization;

- The extent to which efforts should be made to gather information or follow up information with further investigation; and

- The extent of any sanctions or penalties for failing to comply with disclosure requirements.

State statutes regarding the disclosure of nonidentifying information are in flux and, as a result, it is not possible to provide a completely accurate report of all current state disclosure statutes. Examples of three state statutes in effect in 1997, however, are provided in Table 4.

Adoption professionals should consult their state laws regarding the collection and disclosure of health and other background information. These requirements should be addressed by agencies in their current practice. Additionally, judicial decisions to date suggest that courts may be willing to impose liability on agencies in line with existing statutory requirements, even if the law was enacted after the date of the adoption at issue in a wrongful adoption suit. Accordingly, a thorough knowledge of current statutory requirements can assist agencies in assessing potential liability in adoption cases handled prior to enactment of statutory disclosure provisions.

A statutory model for disclosure of health and background information to adoptive parents is provided by the Uniform Adoption Act

(UAA), which has been approved by the National Commission on Uniform State Laws and has been considered by several state legislatures. Although many provisions of the UAA have evoked criticism [Newman 1996; Howe 1995], the provision on the collection and disclosure of health and other background information provides useful guidance on the type of health and other background information that should be collected and communicated.

The UAA requires that a written report be provided to the prospective adoptive parent which contains specific information to the extent that such information is "reasonably available from any person who has had legal or physical custody of the child or who has provided medical, psychological, educational, or similar services to the child." The UAA lists the following required information:

- A current medical and psychological history, including an account of the child's prenatal care; medical condition at birth; any drug or medication taken by the child's mother during pregnancy; any subsequent medical, psychological, or psychiatric examination and diagnosis; any physical, sexual, or emotional abuse suffered by the child; and a record of any immunizations and health care received while in foster or other care.

- Relevant information concerning the medical and psychological history of the child's parents and relatives, including any known disease or hereditary predisposition to disease, any addiction to drugs or alcohol, the health of the child's mother during her pregnancy, and the health of each parent at the child's birth.

- Relevant information concerning the social history of the child and the child's parents and relatives, including
  - the child's enrolment and performance in school, results of educational testing, and any special educational needs;
  - the child's racial, ethnic, and religious background, and a general description of the child's parents; and

## Table 4. Examples of States Statutes Requiring Disclosure of Health and Background Information

| STATE | STATUTORY REQUIREMENTS |
|---|---|
| Texas | Family Code, Section 162.007. Contents of Health, Social, Educational and Genetic History Report<br>The **health history** of the child must include information about:<br>• the child's health status at the time of placement;<br>• the child's birth, neonatal, and other medical, psychological and dental history information;<br>• a record of immunizations for the child; and<br>• the available results of medical, psychological, psychiatric and dental examinations of the child.<br>The **social history** of the child must include information, to the extent known, about past and existing relationships between the child and the child's siblings, parents by birth, extended family, and other persons who have had physical possession of or legal access to the child.<br>The **educational history** of the child must include, to the extent known, information about:<br>• the enrollment and performance of the child in educational institutions;<br>• results of educational testing and standardized tests for the child; and<br>• special educational needs, if any, of the child.<br>The **genetic history** of the child must include a description of the child's parents by birth and their parents, any other child born to either of the child's parents, and extended family members and must include, to the extent the information is available, information about:<br>• their health and medical history, including any genetic diseases and disorders;<br>• their health status at the time of placement;<br>• the cause of and their age at death;<br>• their height, weight, and eye and hair color;<br>• their nationality and ethnic background;<br>• their general levels of educational and professional achievements, if any;<br>• their religious backgrounds, if any;<br>• any psychological, psychiatric, or social evaluations, including the date of the evaluation, any diagnosis, and a summary of findings;<br>• any criminal conviction records relating to a misdemeanor or felony classified as an offense against the person or public decency or a felony violation of a statute intended to control the possession or distribution of a substance included in Chapter 481 of the Health and Safety Code; and<br>• any information necessary to determine whether the child is entitled to or otherwise eligible for state or federal financial, medical or other assistance. |

## Table 4 (continued)

| STATE | STATUTORY REQUIREMENTS |
|---|---|
| Calif. | **Family Code Section 8706**<br>An agency may not place a child for adoption unless a written report on the child's medical background and, if available, the medical background of the child's biological parents so far as ascertainable, has been submitted to the prospective adoptive parents and they have acknowledged in writing the receipt of the report.<br>The report on the child's background shall contain all known diagnostic information, including current medical reports on the child, psychological evaluations and scholastic information as well as all known information regarding the child's developmental history.<br>The biological parents may provide a blood sample at a clinic or hospital approved by the State Department of Health Services. . . . The purpose of the stored sample of blood is to provide a blood sample from which DNA testing can be done at the request of the adoptive parents or the adopted child. The blood sample shall be stored and released in such a manner as to not identify any party to the adoption. Any results of the DNA testing shall be stored and released in such a manner as not to identify any party to the adoption. |
| New Jersey | **Title 9 Juvenile and Domestic Relations Courts**<br>Section 9:3-41.1 Provision of available information on child's development to prospective parent<br>An approved agency making an investigation of the facts and circumstances surrounding the surrender of a child shall provide a prospective parent with all available information, other than information which would identify or permit the identification of the birth parent of the child, relevant to the child's development, including his developmental and medical history, personality and temperament, the parent's complete medical histories, including conditions or diseases which are believed to be hereditary, any drugs or medications taken during pregnancy and any other conditions of the parent's health which may be a factor influencing the child's present or future health. This information shall be made available to the prospective adoptive parent prior to the actual adoptive placement to the extent available and supplemented upon the completion of an investigation conducted by an approved agency . . . |

- an account of the child's past and existing relationship with any individual with whom the child has regularly lived or visited.

• Information concerning a criminal conviction of a parent for a felony, a judicial order terminating the parental rights of a parent, and a proceeding in which the parent was alleged to have abused, neglected, abandoned, or otherwise mistreated the child.

• Information concerning a criminal conviction or delinquency adjudication of the child.

• Information necessary to determine the child's eligibility for state or federal benefits, including subsidies for adoption and other financial, medical, or similar assistance.

# Policy and Practice Issues

## The Scope of the Duty to Disclose

With the increase in wrongful adoption suits, agencies recognize the potential liability they face if they fail to disclose known material health and other background information to prospective adoptive parents. The decisions in *Burr*, *Michael J.*, *Juman*, *Meracle*, *Mallette*, *Caritas*, *Roe*, *Gibbs*, and *Mohr* provide important guidance on the parameters of the duty to disclose in domestic adoptions. The recent international cases likewise provide guidance on disclosure, particularly in relation to the types of written agreements agencies should utilize with prospective adoptive parents. Questions, however, have arisen about the appropriate scope of this duty. Increasingly, writers in the field and practitioners are advocating policies and practices that are asserted to be critical to fulfilling agencies' duty to disclose and to avoiding liability for wrongful adoption. These recommendations warrant close analysis, both from the perspective of the extent to which they promote quality practice, and the extent to which they provide agencies with appropriate guidance in avoiding wrongful adoption liability.

### The Duty to Investigate

Some writers have argued that although no court in a reported opinion to date has recognized a duty to investigate, such a duty should be imposed on agencies to ensure that full and accurate information is gathered and communicated to prospective adoptive parents [Lewis 1992; Blair 1990]. These writers contend that without a duty to investigate, the information that agencies gather will be limited, and agencies will be able to claim that their minimal efforts were sufficient. In the words of one proponent, without imposing the duty to investigate, there is a risk that adoption agencies will take a "see no evil, hear no evil, and say no evil" approach [Blair 1990]. Proponents of a duty to investigate, however, generally have not considered its potential impact on casework with birth families nor the policy and practice implications of implementing an investigation-oriented gathering of information. These considerations are best illustrated by case examples:

> Amy, a 24-year-old birth mother expecting her first child, tells her social worker that she is unsure who the father of her child is. She had relationships with two men at the time she conceived her child, she does not currently have a relationship with either man, and she refuses to name or attempt to make contact with either of them. She is ashamed of the fact that she is uncertain of the identity of her child's father and will not discuss the situation further. Despite her social worker's supportive work with her and explanations about the importance of gathering health and other background information from the birth father, she refuses to divulge any further information.

> Sandy, a 26-year-old birth mother and her boyfriend, 28-year-old Peter, the birth father, provide as much information as they can recall about their own health histories and backgrounds. Both are forthcoming and want to be as helpful as possible, but they are not willing to contact or otherwise involve their families. Peter, whose family lives in Canada and from whom he has been estranged for several years, reports that he remembers his mother saying that her father [Peter's grandfather] was hospitalized for many years for "nerves." He recalls nothing more. He does not want to approach his family to obtain any further information, because he does not want his family to know anything about his current situation.

From a policy and practice perspective, these case examples raise questions about imposing a duty to investigate:

- How much further should adoption agencies go beyond gathering as much information as possible from birth parents? For example, in Amy's case, should the agency pursue outside sources of information to attempt to learn the identity of the birth father—such as interviewing family members, friends, or neighbors or seeking paternity testing by men who may have fathered the child? Should the agency, in Peter's case, contact his family to learn more about his grandfather's history of mental illness?

- Would such investigations violate the privacy of birth parents? When they decide to work with an adoption agency, do birth parents implicitly authorize agencies to gather any information they believe they need (even if the birth parent specifically objects to certain types of inquiries)?

- If agencies were to pursue such investigative efforts against birth parents' wishes, what effect would such a policy have on birth parents' willingness to consider adoption? To what extent would such agency policies cause birth parents to seek the services of independent practitioners who would not make such investigative efforts but who also are not likely to offer the range of counseling and support services offered by agencies?

- Is investigation an appropriate role for adoption social workers who are counseling birth parents?

- How should agency resources be allocated? Should resources be committed to investigative efforts that go beyond work with birth parents? At what point would such an investigation of background information be considered complete? If exhaustive efforts would be required, what impact would such activities have on the length of time a child remains in a temporary setting pending the adoptive placement?

As these questions suggest, imposing a duty to investigate is neither as straightforward as it may appear nor is it as purely beneficial as its advocates would maintain. An investigative approach to the collection of health and other background information may well translate into a standard of practice that would demand the ferreting out of information irrespective of the wishes of birth parents and with limited attention to their privacy interests. Such an approach may well work profound changes in the nature of social work with birth parents by elevating the fact-finding function to a level that makes the psychosocial aspects of the work of secondary value. Birth parents may find such an investigative approach so discomforting—particularly when added to the stresses and complexities inherent in the relinquishment decision—that adoption becomes an even more rarely considered alternative than is currently the case.

Finally, imposing a duty to investigate raises issues about the scope of such a duty. If a duty to investigate were imposed on agencies, how much of an investigative effort would be required and what level of resources should be devoted to meeting that standard? At what point could an agency reasonably conclude its "investigation"? Should it be required to leave "no stone unturned"? And if so, how should the costs of such extensive investigations be met? If the duty to disclose were to expand to exhaustive data gathering, adoption agencies may well find themselves facing expectations that children's future health can be definitively guaranteed. In such a case, adoption agencies would face significant legal risks in connection with virtually every adoptive placement.

### Communicating Facts versus Suspicions

The disclosure of background information also raises questions about the duty to communicate not only known information, but information that adoption social workers may suspect or infer from statements from birth parents. Some agencies report that, out of concerns about failure to disclose and potential wrongful adoption liability, they have made it a practice to inform prospective adoptive parents about any suspected background fact even though unverified. Such practices and their implications are best illustrated by case examples.

> Anne, a 22-year-old birth mother, tells her social worker that she has not drunk any alcohol during her pregnancy. She has been straightforward throughout the counseling and there is no reason to doubt her honesty. However, she also reports that her boyfriend and the father of her child is a

heavy drinker, and she has accompanied him to bars during her pregnancy, although she herself has not had anything to drink. She is clearly dependent on her boyfriend and allows him to make many decisions. The social worker, despite Anne's statements that she has not drunk alcohol, nevertheless classifies the baby as prenatally alcohol involved and potentially affected by Fetal Alcohol Syndrome. That decision significantly reduces the number of prospective adoptive parents interested in adopting the baby and adds to the time the child must remain in foster care.

Cathy's 2-year-old, Tony, has been in foster care for one year and she has, with counseling, decided to relinquish him for adoption. Cathy and her mother, in interviews with the social worker, tell her that the child's father was a transient worker who left town shortly after Cathy became pregnant. Their description of their family life causes the social worker concern. Cathy's father is described as an overbearing, troubled man who was physically abusive of Cathy early in her life but who became far more affectionate toward her once she reached the age of 11. Cathy will not make eye contact with the social worker whenever the subject of her father is raised. The social worker begins to wonder if Cathy's father sexually abused her, and whether Tony is the result of an incestuous relationship. Cathy and her mother vehemently deny any sexual abuse. The social worker, however, decides to be on the safe side and to include in the background information that Tony may have been the product of incest.

From a policy and practice perspective, these case examples raise questions about conveying unverified suspicions in efforts to avoid liability for "wrongful adoption":

- To what extent should the information provided by birth parents be taken at face value? Should the accuracy of the information be questioned based on, for example, assumptions about the birth parent's behavior, as in Anne's case, or on nonverbal behavior, as in Cathy's case?

- Should suspicions, although unverified, be given the same weight as information expressly disclosed by the birth parent? If so, which suspicions should be communicated and which should not? Is it a matter of clinical judgment? Should there be standards about such disclosures?

- Should the impact on a child's opportunities for adoption be taken into account in determining whether to communicate unverified suspicions? When the suspicion relates to significant background information which, if incorrect, would unfairly label a child, is the communication nevertheless appropriate?

These questions reflect the complexities that communication of unverified suspicions entail. When concern about wrongful adoption liability is a primary factor driving disclosure decisions, issues will inevitably arise about whether to fully accept the statements made by birth parents or scrutinize their veracity in light of other information that could suggest a more negative history. Suspicions may be legitimately raised by a variety of factors with no real opportunity to verify those suspicions, and adoption professionals must determine whether or not to include such information as part of the child's health and other background information. Because practice has not addressed the standards to be applied in conveying unverified suspicions about a child's background, such decisions tend to be made on an highly individualized, and, therefore, inconsistent basis.

There may be a tendency to "overdisclose" rather than risk liability later for failing to disclose. Such decision making may not take adequate account of the consequences for children when negative background information is incorrectly ascribed to them. Labeling a child as prenatally alcohol or drug exposed or the product of incest, for example, can diminish the pool of prospective adoptive parents for the child; create limited expectations for the child's future health, wellbeing, and ability to achieve; and adversely affect the child's selfesteem and perceptions of his or her birth family. The desire to fully disclose—and the desire to avoid wrongful adoption liability—should be carefully balanced against the potential negative consequences of disclosing unverified suspicions. Without such a balance, fears of potential legal liability are likely to outweigh standards of quality adoption practice.

## Genetic Testing and the Duty to Disclose

One area in which some writers advocate for greater information gathering and communication is through the genetic testing of children as part of adoption evaluations. These proposals advocate the use of presymptomatic genetic testing to determine the existence of genetic markers for diseases or conditions that the child could develop in the future [Rauch & Rike, n.d.]. One of the benefits attributed to this practice is that it will offer adoption agencies greater insulation against wrongful adoption suits [Rauch & Rike, n.d.]. This proposed use of genetic testing generally has not taken into account the ethical considerations that presymptomatic testing raises, nor the potential danger of creating new standards of practice against which agency liability would be determined. The issues are best illustrated by case examples:

> Baby Sam is an apparently healthy newborn with no known family history of Huntington's Disease. The couple considering adopting him has become aware from recent news reports that there is a test that can be done to determine whether an individual has the genetic marker for Huntington's Disease. They have requested that the test be done on Sam, even though there is no indication that he is at risk for the disease. They would like this information before making the final decision to adopt Sam.

> Three-year-old Lakesha, in foster care since she was only a few months old, has had a complete family and medical history. There is no indication of a family history of either alcoholism or mental illness. The couple considering adopting Lakesha, however, are concerned about the physical abuse that led to her coming into foster care and worry that, despite the history that has been taken, there may be substance abuse or mental health problems in her birth family. They have read that there are now tests for genetic markers for

alcoholism and certain mental illnesses. As a precaution, they would like Lakesha tested. They state that they do not think the test results would be a factor in their decision to adopt her, but nonetheless, would like to know whether she is genetically predisposed to these conditions.

Tommy, age 4, and Timmy, age 2, are being considered for adoption by Mr. and Mrs. Green, who ask that genetic testing be conducted on both boys to determine whether they are carriers of the gene for cystic fibrosis (CF). There is no reported history of cystic fibrosis in the birth family. Mrs. Green had a cousin who died as a child from CF, and the couple feels that the information will help them to decide whether or not to adopt the boys. The agency agrees to their request, and the tests are conducted. Tommy is found to be a carrier and Timmy is not. The couple then state that they wish to adopt Timmy, but do not feel emotionally prepared to adopt Tommy given his carrier status.

From a policy and practice perspective, these case examples raise a number of troubling issues about the use of presymptomatic genetic testing as part of the adoption evaluation of a child. These issues demonstrate that support for genetic testing on the grounds of avoiding liability for wrongful adoption must take into account critical ethical considerations that bear on such decision making:

- Should agencies be willing to conduct presymptomatic genetic testing of apparently healthy children solely at the request of prospective adoptive families?

- To what extent should decisions about presymptomatic genetic testing take into account the interests and rights of the child?

- What are the implications for children when presymptomatic genetic testing reveals genetic predispositions for significant, but nontreatable, conditions such as Huntington's Disease?

- What are the implications for siblings when one child is found to be genetically desirable and the other is not, and decisions to adopt are made on that basis?

These issues reflect the significant ethical issues that presymptomatic genetic testing raises issues which, when weighed against advice to use such testing to "prevent 'wrongful adoption' " [Rauch & Rike, n.d.], counsel against a policy that embraces ready use of such testing. Recommendations to use genetic testing to alleviate the anxieties of prospective adoptive families and shield adoption agencies from potential liability often ignore the interests of children who are subjected to such testing. The ethical considerations include the impact of such testing on the future well-being of children and the extent to which such testing violates children's rights to privacy and their rights to consent to testing that may reveal serious and untreatable diseases and to make personal decisions about what they wish and do not wish to know about themselves [Freundlich, in press]. Full account must be taken of the harmful effects on children that may result from presymptomatic genetic testing. The implementation of such testing as part of an adoption evaluation should be carefully examined, particularly when testing is being considered solely based on concerns about wrongful adoption liability.

Not only can the implementation of genetic testing as part of adoption evaluations fail to take into account critical ethical considerations, but it can lead to the creation of a standard of practice that could be used by courts to assess whether agencies properly disclosed relevant and material information. Literature that counsels agencies to incorporate "state-of-the-art genetic testing" in evaluating children for adoption [Rauch & Rike, n.d.] should, as a result, be approached with great caution. Implementing such recommendations may inadvertently lead to a new standard against which agencies could be judged subsequently by courts in wrongful adoption suits. Ironically, by proposing the use of presymptomatic genetic testing as a way to avoid wrongful adoption liability, the field may in fact be creating an additional basis on which wrongful adoption liability may be imposed.

## Disclosing Facts versus Interpretative Information

An area of concern for many adoption professionals who desire to communicate the full information to prospective adoptive families is the extent to which interpretative information about background facts should be conveyed. The issues related to the disclosure of facts versus interpretive information can best be illustrated by case examples:

> Ms. Adams is interested in adopting $1\frac{1}{2}$-year-old Sherri who was prenatally exposed to cocaine. The social workers have fully informed Ms. Adams about Sherri's background, and Ms. Adams wants to know what the long-term outcomes are likely to be for Sherri's health and development. The social workers are aware that the research shows different outcomes, depending on a range of factors. They are not certain which articles and research they should provide to Ms. Adams to give her the most complete information.

> Mr. and Mrs. Brooks are interested in adopting 6-year-old Jerry whose family history includes a number of mental health problems: his grandmother was considered "high-strung," his grandfather had a "drinking problem," and his mother seemed to have had periods of depression. The agency has provided Mr. and Mrs. Brooks with this information, and the couple asks their social worker what the probability is that Jerry will develop mental health problems later. The social worker is not certain and wonders whether to research this issue and advise Mr. and Mrs. Brooks accordingly.

As these cases demonstrate, prospective adoptive parents often seek to better understand the background information they are given and may press adoption professionals to interpret the information that has been provided. While some professionals have advised workers to "include best guesses" [Donley 1990: 9], the wrongful adoption cases counsel against such a practice. As the *Meracle* case best illustrates, imparting inaccurate information (in that case, a child's chances of developing Huntington's Disease) can subject an agency to liability. Staff generally should not offer interpretative information but instead should refer prospective adoptive parents to independent experts and other resources with the requisite expertise.

## The Duty to Provide Updated Information

An issue that agencies often face relates to communication of health and other background information acquired after an adoption is finalized. Although some states have established central registries that allow birth parents to provide updated health information, neither these statutes nor wrongful adoption case law imposes a legal duty on agencies to provide adoptive families with information obtained after the adoption has been finalized. In the absence of a legal duty, the question becomes whether the agency has a professional responsibility to provide adoptive families with information acquired after finalization. The implications of such a duty are best illustrated by case examples.

> The maternal grandmother of an infant placed for adoption more than a year ago calls her daughter's social worker to say that the father of the infant has had a chronic serious drinking problem and has recently entered an alcohol rehabilitation program. The birth father was not involved in the placement other than to sign the necessary legal documents, and neither the birth mother nor any member of her family provided any information on the birth father's alcohol problem. This information is the first indication of any alcohol-related problem in the child's background.

> Ms. Davis surrendered a child to the agency for adoption seven years ago. The child was placed with a family who requested that a healthy, Anglo American, or Hispanic infant be placed with them. Ms. Davis recently telephoned the social worker to say that she had just learned from a mutual acquaintance that the child's birth father was not Hispanic, as she had assumed, but was of African American heritage and that he recently had learned that he carried the gene for sickle cell anemia.

These case examples raise a range of issues regarding the approach that agencies should take in determining whether to disclose health and other background information acquired after finalization:

- Should agencies automatically communicate any information provided to them after the adoption has been finalized? Should efforts be made first to verify the accuracy of the information and the reliability of the source, such as the case of information on the birth father provided by the birth mother's family?

- Should decisions to communicate updated information depend upon the nature of the information? Should there be a greater responsibility to communicate information about life-threatening conditions than about other types of medical problems? Alternatively, should the decision to disclose turn on whether the condition has genetic implications? In the context of a genetically transmitted condition, should disclosure depend on whether knowledge of the condition would facilitate diagnosis and/or treatment? How should "developmental" information be treated as opposed to purely medical? Are more specifically diagnosed illnesses and conditions, such as dyslexia, more critical to disclose than general problems, such as unspecified learning difficulties?

- Should an agency disclose to the adoptive family new information about the child's background that is not strictly health related, such as information pertaining to the child's race? Should disclosure depend on an assessment of the adoptive parents' ability to accept this information without any detriment to the child? Should it make a difference in the agency's decision to disclose if there are medical implications associated with a different racial or ethnic background, as in the case example?

- Should agencies have a policy of routinely disclosing any updated information to adoptive families or, alternatively, a policy of informing adoptive families when updated information becomes available, permitting the family to decide if they wish to receive it?

These questions raise some of the many considerations that agencies are likely to face when receiving updated health and other background information after finalization. Some agencies have developed standards in this area, but practice varies significantly. One approach is to disclose any information that appears reliable if it pertains to a physical or psychological condition or illness that could directly affect the present or future health of the child. At the other end of the spectrum, some agencies communicate only updated information on medical conditions or illnesses for which screening and treatment are available. Although each of these approaches provides a useful framework, the complexity of the issues may not be fully addressed by either standard of practice. In the absence of a legally defined duty in this area, agencies are faced with the challenge, as well as the opportunity, to define practice in a way that conforms with professional social work standards and takes into account the interests and needs of all members of the triad.

## Another Aspect of Wrongful Adoption: Complaints of Wrongful Placement by Adopted Individuals

In contrast to wrongful adoption claims by adoptive families, relatively little legal attention has been given to wrongful placement claims by adopted individuals. Reports from the field, however, indicate that such claims are becoming more common. In a number of cases, adopted individuals have returned to agencies with complaints that the agency should not have placed them with their adoptive families, because the agency knew or should have known of problems within those families. Often, the individual recounts painful or traumatic childhood experiences of abuse or neglect by the adoptive parents and asserts that the harm suffered was the result of the agency's negligence in approving the family for adoption and placement of the individual with the family. Commonly, the adopted individual claims that the agency failed to take reasonable steps to investigate the prospective adoptive family's background, or that the agency had information about the adoptive family which should have put the agency on notice that the family was not suitable to adopt. In those cases that have advanced to the filing of litigation, adopted individuals typically have sought money damages to compensate them for emotional pain and suffering and the costs of psychological and other services that they have obtained and/or will need in the future.

Because these cases have been settled by the parties before a judicial determination was reached, it is not clear whether courts will recognize a cause of action brought by adopted individuals for wrongful placement. It is reasonable to anticipate, however, given the legal developments in relation to wrongful adoption on behalf of adoptive families, that courts will recognize the right of adopted individuals to seek redress if they have been harmed as a result of agency misconduct in placing them with their adoptive families.

There may be important differences, however, between these cases and "wrongful adoption" cases brought by adoptive families. First, it is likely that wrongful placement suits on behalf of adopted individuals will be based on negligence rather than on theories of intentional misconduct. The complaint is likely to be that agencies failed to use due care in the evaluation process, rather than that agencies deliberately selected an inappropriate family for a child. Second, the thrust of the complaint of adopted individuals will not be a failure to disclose material information but, instead, a failure to make appropriate placement decisions. Wrongful placement suits brought by adoptees are likely to present a wide range of issues not present in wrongful adoption suits brought by adoptive families. The evaluation of the adoptive family is likely to be called into question, including what the agency asked and did not ask, what information the prospective adoptive parents did and did not provide, and how the agency interpreted and assessed the information. The selection process will also be closely examined in any litigation, especially the factors employed by the agency in matching a child with a family.

Determinations of agency liability under a negligence standard will be further complicated by the fact that it will require the use of the prevailing standard of practice at the time the evaluation of the prospective adoptive parents took place. Because practice in this area has changed significantly over the past decades, the determination and application of the prevailing standard of practice at the time the placement decision was made may present difficult issues. Agencies should be aware that courts, in examining records about adoptive families, likely will consider whether sufficient information was obtained to make an appropriate assessment and whether there were indications of future problems. Assessments of prospective adoptive families completed in past decades are likely to lack much of the information that would be included in contemporary home studies to fully assess parenting capacity. It may well be that certain questions were not asked and certain procedures, such as criminal record or child abuse registry checks that are standard under current practice, were not conducted. Although these omissions may be understandable in light of standards of practice at the time the assessments were conducted, they may also raise questions about past practice that agencies find difficult to fully explain.

Agencies that have faced the possibility of a lawsuit by an adopted individual point out that the complaint often involves abuse or other harm at the hands of the adoptive parent years after the adoption is finalized. This passage of time raises significant questions that are not easily resolved. How long should an agency remain responsible for a child's well-being after the adoption is finalized? Is an agency, for example, responsible if an adoptive parent physically abuses the child she adopted five years after the adoption? Is an agency responsible if an adoptive parent subsequently marries a man who sexually abuses the child?

In light of adopted individuals' complaints that have come to light thus far, some agencies have expressed concerns that current policies promoting transracial adoption and recent mandates related to the Americans with Disabilities Act may lead to claims by adopted individuals. With regard to transracial adoption policies, the concern is that adoptees may later claim that adoptive placements outside their communities of color have harmed them [Oppenheim 1997]. Federal law, as stated in the Interethnic Adoption Provisions of the Small Business Job Protection Act of 1996, essentially prohibits the consideration of race, culture, or ethnicity in a foster or adoptive placement [Office for Civil Rights and Administration for Children and Families 1997]. Will agencies, conforming to these mandates, later face liability if an African American child adopted by an Anglo American family, for example, asserts that he or she was harmed by being deprived of a family and community of his or her own race and culture? If an individual attributes mental health problems to his transracial adoption, will the agency potentially have liability under a theory of wrongful placement? Although speculative at this point, there are aspects of transracial adoption practice that may have implications related to "wrongful adoption," issues that should be carefully considered as policies in this area are developed and implemented.

In addition to the federal requirements related to transracial adoption practice, there are federal legislative requirements in the Americans with Disabilities Act of 1990 (ADA) that also raise concerns related to potential wrongful adoption liability. The ADA broadly protects individuals with disabilities from discrimination in the workplace, as well as in relation to services provided by certain "public accommodations," such as adoption agencies.

The ADA prohibits adoption agencies from, on the basis of agency policy and practice, rejecting individuals as prospective adoptive parents by reason of an actual or perceived disability. Protected disabilities under the ADA broadly include physical diseases, handicapping conditions, and mental illnesses and disorders. Although agencies are permitted to conduct individualized assessments to determine whether, on the basis of safety, an individual with a disability should qualify as an adoptive parent, there are, nonetheless, risks associated with decisions to reject applicants based on disability. Agencies potentially face charges of discrimination and litigation based on alleged violations of the ADA when they reject applicants on the basis of disability [Freundlich 1997]. Potential liability under the ADA appears to exist even when agencies inquire about applicants' health and other history in an effort to comply with state laws that require prospective adoptive parents to be in reasonably good health as a prerequisite to adopting.

The implications of the ADA mandates in relation to potential wrongful adoption liability are best illustrated by case examples.

> Mr. and Mrs. Smith apply to the agency to adopt a healthy newborn. Mr. Smith admits to having used intravenous drugs while in his late teens and early twenties. Now 29, he states that he has not used illegal drugs for six years. Mr. Smith voluntarily discloses that he contracted HIV as a result of

his intravenous drug use. Mrs. Smith does not volunteer any information about her HIV status, and by law, the agency may not seek this information. The agency is concerned that Mr. Smith's history of past drug use and his current HIV status and the uncertainty about Mrs. Smith's status raise serious issues in relation to adoptive parenting. The agency is concerned that a child placed with the Smiths may not have the benefit of a family over the long term and would prefer not to approve the family. The agency, however, is aware that the ADA includes within protected disabilities past drug use and, as interpreted by the U.S. Justice Department, HIV infection, and that rejecting the Smiths on this basis may subject the agency to an ADA complaint. They wonder if later, a child placed with the Smiths might assert that the agency should not have placed him with parents who died prematurely or were severely and chronically ill as a result of disabilities.

Ms. Jones, age 36, applies to the agency to adopt a child from Eastern Europe or Russia. Although she has been gainfully employed for 10 years, she admits to having fought depression since she was a teenager. She shares with the social worker that she has been twice hospitalized for attempting suicide, once during her freshman year of college and most recently four years ago after the death of her mother. During this most recent hospitalization, she took a three-month leave from her job. She is on medication and her therapist feels that her condition is at present under control. The agency is concerned about Ms. Jones' psychiatric history but is aware that mental illness is a protected disability under the ADA and rejection of Ms. Jones could result in a discrimination complaint.

Mr. and Mrs. Day apply to a adopt a child who has Fetal Alcohol Syndrome and Attention Deficit Hyperactivity Disorder. Mrs. Day has Multiple Sclerosis (MS) and is confined to a wheelchair. Mr. Day is in good health and has played an important role in supporting Mrs. Day's efforts to lead a productive life. The home is fully adapted and the Days have an extended network of friends and family. The agency previously had a policy under which they refused to consider any adoptive applicant with MS and who was wheelchair-bound. With the passage of the ADA, the agency is aware that it must reconsider this policy, but it continues to have grave concerns about the appropriateness of approving an applicant with these types of physical disabilities. The agency worries about the present and future care that a child may receive and the possibility that a child placed with the Days may later claim that the placement was not an appropriate one.

Ms. Browne, whose baby is due in three months, is working closely with the agency to select the adoptive family for her child. The agency has approved a range of families, including one couple in which the wife is currently in remission for cancer and whose prognosis is good and another couple in which the husband is significantly overweight. Ms. Browne does not wish to give either couple any consideration as she wants a "perfectly healthy" family for her child. The agency is finding that birth mothers involved in the selection process increasingly are not willing to consider families with health problems.

These cases illustrate the complex legal issues that face agencies as they make determinations related to the approval and selection of applicants who are protected by the ADA. On the one hand, there are concerns about potential liability to applicants for wrongfully rejecting them as adoptive parents, and on the other, there are concerns about potential liability later if a child adopted by an individual with disabilities asserts that he or she was harmed as a result of the placement. These issues are further complicated by the growing practice of involving birth parents in the selection of the adoptive family for their child. If, for example, a birth parent rejects a prospective adoptive parent because of a disability, does the agency remain potentially liable to the applicant under the ADA? On the other hand, if a birth parent knowingly chooses an adoptive parent who has a significant physical or mental health problem, does the agency nevertheless remain potentially liable to the adopted individual who later claims wrongful placement? These complexities are likely to continue to present quandaries for agencies as they weigh the demands of the ADA, professional considerations related to child-focused adoption placement practice, and issues related to wrongful adoption placement claims of adult adoptees.

# Recommendations
# for Practice

The law on wrongful adoption provides guidance on the duty of agencies and independent practitioners to disclose health and other background information to prospective adoptive parents. The cases and state disclosure statutes make clear that liability will be imposed if agencies fail to disclose known material health and other background information about a child and the child's birth family. Agencies may not misrepresent the child's background, portraying it as more favorable than the agency knows it to be, nor may agencies deliberately conceal unfavorable information. Agencies are also required, at a minimum, to communicate known information if asked by prospective adoptive parents and, when volunteering information, to impart known information fully and accurately. Expanding on that requirement, some courts recently have imposed a duty on agencies to provide all material health and other background information in the agency's possession, irrespective of whether the prospective adoptive parents specifically ask for that information or whether the agency prefers to remain silent.

Although the cases and statutes provide important guidance, there are areas in which the scope of the duty to disclose is not clear. Case law to date has not clarified, for example, what may be required of agencies when health and other background information in agency files is scanty; what agencies must do in relation to pursuing information in order to present as complete and accurate a history as is possible, although no reported case has imposed a duty to investigate; when the background information appears complete, what efforts, if any, an agency must take to verify the completeness and accuracy of the information in its possession; or, when agencies receive information postplacement, what their obligations are to communicate that information. There are a number of steps, however, that agencies may take to ensure quality practice in disclosing health and other background information and, thereby, limit their exposure to liability for wrongful adoption even in light of this uncertainty. Attention to issues related to insurance coverage for potential wrongful adoption liability is also critical to an agency's planning and practice in this area.

## Practice Recommendations

Agencies can improve practice and limit exposure to wrongful adoption liability by taking steps in the following areas:

- Obtaining and disclosing material health and other background information,

- Educating prospective adoptive parents about the limits on information gathering and disclosure,

- Heightening adoptive parents' awareness about their own responsibilities in reaching an informed decision about whether to adopt a particular child,

- Providing adoptive parents with written disclosure of health and other background information and with documents that describe the risks and uncertainties associated with adoption, and

- Staff training.

### Obtaining and Disclosing Material Health and Other Background Information

Agencies should use the concept of "materiality" to guide the collection and disclosure of health and other background information. Material information is any information that may be important to a prospective adoptive parent in deciding whether to adopt a particular child. It is the failure to disclose this type of information that deprives prospective adoptive parents of an opportunity to make an informed decision and that places agencies at risk of liability for wrongful adoption. Agencies should have processes in place to ensure that material information is obtained from birth families and is communicated to prospective adoptive parents.

Collection of material health and other background information involves work with birth parents to elicit, through counseling and sensitive questioning, medical history, family background, and other information bearing on the child's health and developmental status. In addition to interviews with birth parents, there are specific strategies that agencies can use to enhance the quality and reliability of the health and other background information they obtain. Specifically with regard to collection of health information, agencies may use birth parent medical questionnaires, obtain and review hospital and other health care records, and ensure that children have physical examinations immediately prior to placement. Agencies should also develop clear policies and guidelines on collection and disclosure of social and family background information and disclosure of information on children's HIV status.

### *Health Information*

**Birth Parent Medical Questionnaires.** Agencies should develop standardized forms that guide the collection of information from birth families about a child's health status and history. The content of these forms should incorporate any information that state disclosure laws mandate and include, at a minimum, the specific areas listed in the CWLA Standards related to the child's health status and the birth family's health history. The questions in these forms should be framed to elicit and therefore facilitate the sharing of the fullest information possible. For example, rather than asking a birth mother, "Did you take any drugs during your pregnancy?" the question might be posed more neutrally as, "Which drugs did you take during your pregnancy?"

Birth parents should sign medical questionnaires and agencies should have all questionnaires notarized. These formalities convey the importance of the information contained in the questionnaires and encourage birth parents to respond thoughtfully and thoroughly. Agencies should note on each questionnaire who provided the information: the birth mother, the birth father, or another member of the birth family. If the birth mother completes the questionnaire for both herself and the birth father, she should so indicate on the form.

Social workers should compare the information in medical questionnaires to case record narratives that describe their interviews with birth parents and note any inconsistencies in the documented information. They should attempt to reconcile any differences and, when necessary, recontact birth parents for further information. When staff are unable to reconcile inconsistencies, they should advise prospective adoptive parents of this fact.

Social workers should provide prospective adoptive parents with a copy of the completed medical questionnaire when prospective adoptive parents indicate a readiness to seriously consider the child for adoption. Providing this information at this stage gives prospective adoptive parents a reasonable opportunity to review the information, ask questions, and make an informed decision about adopting the child. The adoptive parents should sign the questionnaire, acknowledging receipt. The document should contain a clearly displayed statement that the agency makes no representation as to the completeness and accuracy of the information.

**Hospital and/or Health Records.** Obtaining hospital and/or health records is a key step toward assuring that material health information is collected. Obtaining information in hospital and/or health records presents different issues depending on whether the adoption is domestic or international, or the adoption is one of a child in foster care. In all cases, however, consents to the release of hospital and health records should be obtained from birth parents, legal guardians, or others required by law to authorize the release of such information.

Agencies that place infants for adoption domestically should obtain all material medical information related to the child's birth, including, if possible, the birth mother's own hospital record. At a minimum, adoptive parents should be given a written summary of information on the labor and delivery, any complications that arose during or immediately after birth, any concerns about the child's health or development that were identified, and the child's medical course prior to hospital discharge. When a written summary is provided, it should contain a statement that the information has been summarized from hospital records and, as in the birth parent medical questionnaires, that the agency makes no representations as to whether the information is complete and accurate.

Agencies should also request from the hospital complete medical records on the birth mother and child. These documents often will be voluminous and contain numerous references to the birth mother's full name and the child's original surname. In those cases in which the birth mother has not waived confidentiality, agencies may choose one of two courses of action in sharing medical records with prospective adoptive parents. Agencies may redact all identifying information and provide the complete records to the adoptive parents to share with their pediatrician or other health care provider. Alternatively, if the agency has a pediatrician on staff or on retainer, the agency may have the physician review the records and, in turn, communicate the information to the prospective adoptive parents or to their pediatrician or other health care provider. If the agency has not received complete medical records prior to placement, it should alert prospective adoptive parents of that fact and offer them the opportunity to delay placement until the records are received. If adoptive parents prefer to proceed with the placement in the absence of complete hospital records, the agency should ask the adoptive parents to sign a written waiver acknowledging their decision to do so.

In international adoptions, medical records often will be unavailable or available in summary form only to the agency prior to placement and, as a result, the agency may have limited information on a child's health and developmental status and history. This situation should be clearly explained orally and in writing to prospective adoptive parents. In some instances, medical records will be available in the country of origin and in these cases, adoptive parents who travel to the child's country should be counseled to ask that these records be provided and translated by a medical professional into English. The agency, however, should inform prospective adoptive parents that there are no guarantees regarding the completeness and accuracy of the medical records that they receive in the child's country. Specifically, adoptive parents should be told that any diagnosis contained in medical records should be re-evaluated for accuracy and that assumptions should be not be made about the absence of any notation about other diagnoses.

For adoption of children in foster care, agencies should obtain, to the maximum extent possible, health care records related to the child's health and developmental status and history before the child's entry into foster care and the child's health care and development while in foster care. This health care information should contain any history of abuse or neglect and any health, mental health, or developmental problems that the child has had or for which he or she is currently receiving care. The information, at a minimum, should be provided in written summary form to the prospective adoptive family with cautionary language regarding the completeness and accuracy of the information. Adoptive parents should sign to acknowledge receipt.

**Physical Examinations of Children.** Physical examinations of children provide important information for adoptive families. The issues related to physical examinations vary somewhat, depending on the type of adoption.

In domestic adoptions of infants, all children should have physical examinations prior to placement with adoptive families. Children should be examined by a pediatrician ideally within 24 hours prior to placement. If a pediatrician is not available or an examination cannot otherwise take place, the adoptive parents should be given the option of delaying the child's placement or, if they choose to go forward, asked to sign a written waiver regarding the examination.

In international adoptions, agencies should inform prospective adoptive families that in many countries of origin, pediatric services do not offer comprehensive physical and developmental evaluations of children. Agencies should attempt to obtain information related to any physical examinations of children that have been completed. Agencies should encourage adoptive parents who travel to the child's country to attempt to supplement existing information with any additional medical or developmental assessments that have been completed.

Because screening and diagnostic pediatric services in many countries are limited and medical records may be incomplete or inaccurate, there is a heightened need for comprehensive evaluations of children by pediatricians who have an understanding of health issues affecting children adopted from abroad. Agencies should encourage adoptive parents to seek professional guidance in assessing the medical and developmental status of children whom they are considering for adoption, including providing medical experts of their choosing with any snapshots or videotapes of the child that are available. Upon the child's arrival in the United States, adoptive parents should have a comprehensive medical and developmental assessment of the child to determine whether there are any health-related problems associated with conditions in the child's country of origin; pursue complete routine tests and procedures, including immunizations, that may not have been performed in the child's country; and have the child's physician determine whether tests and procedures conducted abroad should be repeated. For internationally adopted children who were institutionalized in orphanages at early ages, there may be serious and multiple developmental delays that will require specialized evaluations and services.

For children in foster care, agencies should have pediatric examinations completed when children become available for adoption, and this information should be supplemented and/or updated prior to the child's adoptive placement. Once adoption is the plan for the child, a comprehensive pediatric examination should detail the child's health status, past and current health care needs, and any existing physical, emotional or developmental disabilities. This information, critical to an understanding of the child's needs and the type of family who can best meet those needs, also serves as a basis for determining the child's eligibility for state and federal benefits, including adoption subsidies and other financial or medical support. This information should be supplemented shortly before the child's placement with his or her adoptive family to ensure that the agency and the family have as full an understanding as possible of the child's current health status and needs.

### Collection of Social and Family Background Information

As with health status and history, information related to a child's social and family background should be obtained by agencies and communicated to prospective adoptive parents at the time they consider a child for adoption. A child's social and family background information, which may include both positive attributes of the family as well as issues that indicate problems within the birth family, enables adoptive parents to make a fully informed decision about adoption. This information also provides the child's history that adoptive parents can later share in response to the child's questions about his or her background.

The nature and extent of available social and family background information may vary, depending on the individual case as well as on the domestic or international nature of the adoption. Agencies, however, should make every effort to collect and communicate in writing to prospective adoptive parents information that describes the child's social and family history; social and family problems experienced by the birth family, particularly in relation to the child; and positive attributes of the birth family, such as skills, interests, and aptitudes that would be important to the child's sense of identity and history. Agencies should retain copies of the child's social and family background information to share with adoptees who may return as adults seeking to have the information shared with them by their adoptive families confirmed, clarified, or expanded.

### An Area of Special Concern: Information on a Child's HIV Status

Many agencies, in considering issues related to obtaining and effectively communicating background information, express concerns about disclosure of a child's HIV status to prospective adoptive families. There has been much debate about the propriety of such disclosures. On the one hand, it is argued that prospective adoptive parents have the right to know the child's HIV status just as they should be informed of any other potentially debilitating condition. On the other hand, it is argued that such a disclosure is a breach of confidentiality, imparting to the prospective adoptive parents the likelihood that the birth mother is herself HIV positive and violating the birth mother's and the child's right to privacy.

In most states, child welfare agencies are legally required to disclose a child's HIV status when prospective adoptive parents indicate a willingness to consider the child for adoption [Merkel-Holguin 1996]. This legal requirement corresponds with good practice that, likewise, directs disclosure to prospective adoptive parents. Disclosure of a child's HIV status provides prospective adoptive families with an opportunity to assess their capacity to meet the needs of the child and to prepare themselves to respond to the medical and emotional demands that accompany HIV infection. Notifying the adoptive family of the child's HIV positive status helps ensure that the child receives needed diagnostic and treatment services, and disclosure supports the negotiation of an appropriate adoption subsidy and qualification for other state and federal benefits [National Adoption Information Clearinghouse 1991]. When an agency fails to disclose such information, it places itself at substantial risk both in terms of potentially violating state law, as well as exposing itself to wrongful adoption liability by failing to disclose material information.

To the extent that a child's HIV status is known to an agency, disclosure to prospective adoptive parents is clearly appropriate and, depending on the state, it may be mandated. What is more problematic for agencies is how to proceed when a child's HIV status is not known. Federal and state antidiscrimination legislation prevent agencies from mandating HIV testing, and some states prohibit any party from even inquiring of another whether he or she has had an HIV test. As a result, adoption agencies generally cannot require HIV testing of birth parents, although they can strongly encourage birth parents to seek such testing. When children are in an agency's custody, the question becomes whether children should be HIV tested and the results of these tests communicated to the prospective adoptive parents. The Child Welfare League of America, in its guidelines, advises against mandatory testing of all children, recommending instead an assessment of each individual child's risk of HIV infection and a determination of whether HIV testing is indicated in the particular case [Merkel-Holguin 1996]. The risk factors that should be taken into consideration in deciding whether to test a child are listed in Table 5. In those instances in which an individualized assessment indicates that HIV testing is appropriate, the test should be conducted and the results should be conveyed to prospective adoptive parents considering the child for adoption.

A wrongful adoption suit filed in 1996 against a New York adoption agency highlights the importance of disclosing information that may suggest that a child is at risk of HIV, as well as disclosing a child's positive HIV status whenever known. In *Moreau v. The Roman Catholic Diocese of New York* [1996], the adoptive parent of a child adopted in 1984 and diagnosed with HIV in 1994, asserted that the adoption agency did not disclose that the birth mother abused cocaine and heroin

## Table 5. Risk Factors for HIV Infection in Children

A child is considered at risk for HIV infection if the child or the child's parent(s) meet any of the following criteria:
- Uses or has used intravenous drugs.
- Has or had multiple sexual partners and engaged in unsafe sexual behaviors.
- Engages or engaged in sexual activity with individuals who are or have been involved in risky behaviors, such as intravenous drug use.
- Received blood transfusions before March 1985.
- Has hemophilia and received blood transfusions or blood products before March 1985.
- In the case of a child, was born or breast-fed by his/her mother who was HIV positive.

Reprinted from L. Merkel-Holguin, *Children who lose their parents to HIV / AIDS: Agency guidelines for adoptive and kinship placement* (Washington, DC: CWLA Press), with permission of author.

throughout pregnancy or that the child tested positive for both drugs at birth. The adoptive parent further asserted that the agency did not communicate a medical recommendation that the child receive regular medical assessments at a specialized clinic [Lii 1998]. The adoptive parent argued that had she been advised of the recommendation, she would have ensured that her son was regularly evaluated as recommended. She contended that these medical assessments, if conducted, could have resulted in an early diagnosis of her son's HIV status and prompt treatment of his condition [Lii 1998]. The case, which in early 1998 was still pending, raises questions about agencies' responsibilities in relation to communicating the HIV status or susceptibility of a child adopted in the early to mid-1980s when AIDS first began to surface and transmission was not well understood. Irrespective of how that question may be decided by the court, however, the case emphasizes, as have other wrongful adoption cases, the importance of communicating known medical information and recommendations that may have implications for a child's future health and well being.

The issue of HIV testing of children is likely to be less complicated in the future. The 1996 re-authorization of the Ryan White AIDS Care Act placed new requirements on states to test newborns for HIV and conditioned Ryan White funding in the future on increased rates of HIV testing of pregnant women and substantially decreased rates of HIV among newborns. This policy thrust is likely to result in states implementing mandatory HIV testing of all newborns over the next several years, a development that may help to simplify issues relating to determinations of children's HIV status.

## Educating Prospective Adoptive Parents About the Limits on Information Gathering and Disclosure

Agencies can further enhance practice and limit their exposure to wrongful adoption liability by explaining to prospective adoptive parents that there are limits on the extent to which health and other background information may be fully and accurately obtained. Agencies should clarify that in virtually every case there is information that the agency may not know. In each individual case, an agency should identify any areas in which information is missing with regard to the child's health or social or family background and explain that the information that is available may not be entirely accurate.

Prospective adoptive parents should be helped to understand how health and other background information is obtained. In the case of domestic infant adoptions, they should be told that usually the sole source of information concerning children is the birth parents and, in many cases, only the birth mother. Birth parents may be reluctant to share certain information about family medical or mental health history. In other instances, the information they have may be limited if only because their own parents (the adoptee's biological grandparents) are relatively young and not yet affected by many of the conditions associated with middle age. In international adoptions, the prospective adoptive parents should be helped to understand that the sole source of information is the agency in the sending country, which may have limited access to health and social information about a child.

For adoptions of children in foster care, health and other background information likewise may be limited. Pre-foster care information must generally be gathered from birth families, and information on children's health histories and experiences while they are in foster care may also be less than complete. Although many public child welfare agencies have made great strides, many others struggle with developing and implementing processes that ensure full collection, maintenance, and communication of health and other background information about children in care.

## Heightening Adoptive Parents' Awareness of Their Own Responsibilities

A third area in which agencies can enhance practice in the area of information disclosure is through educating prospective adoptive parents about their own roles and responsibilities in the process. As a starting point, agencies should clearly communicate to prospective adoptive parents that there are risks inherent in adoption, just as there are risks in any form of parenting. Prospective adoptive parents should be helped to understand that, by pursing adoption, they will be assuming responsibilities for which there are no guarantees of specific results or outcomes. Key to practice in this area is communicating to prospective adoptive parents that notwithstanding an agency's best efforts to obtain and disclose health and other background information, it is not possible to provide an assurance that all existing information has been discovered nor is it possible to predict the future health status of a child.

In addition, agencies should encourage prospective adoptive parents to ask for all available information concerning a child's health status and history, developmental status, social history, and birth family background. They should note and question agencies about any significant information that is unclear, conflicting, or missing, including any information gaps in the birth parent medical questionnaires. Prospective adoptive parents should pursue, with the agency and with appropriate experts, any information that indicates a medical, mental health, or developmental problem or signals that there is a risk that a child may later develop such a problem.

Prospective adoptive parents should anticipate that some of the information they receive about a child's background may be difficult to hear. Families may need help in realistically assessing the significance of a child's problems and in honestly assessing their own financial and emotional ability and readiness to respond to and cope with the child's problems. Families should be encouraged to seek information and guidance from a range of resources, including medical experts and adoptive parents of similarly situated children.

## *Providing Adoptive Parents with Written Disclosure of Health and Other Background Information and with Documents That Describe the Risks and Uncertainties Associated with Adoption*

Agencies should provide adoptive parents with written information on the health and social background of the child and ensure that adoptive parents sign, acknowledging receipt of the information. Whenever possible, agencies should provide copies of reports, assessments, or other documentation contained in other records, rather than summarizing material. Summaries tend to include interpretations of the meaning or significance of the information and increase the likelihood of errors in transcription. When materials are provided to prospective adoptive parents on multiple pages, the adoptive parents should initial each page, indicating that they have reviewed the entire document.

In addition to disclosing health and other background information itself, it is important that agencies clearly communicate to prospective adoptive parents certain cautions related to proceeding to adopt on the basis of known health and other background information. Providing these caveats in writing reiterates for adoptive parents the risks and uncertainties involved in adoption and, at the same time, helps to protect agencies from claims of wrongful adoption. Adoptive parents should be provided with the following information in writing and should be asked to sign, acknowledging that this information has been provided to them.

- **The agency is able to provide only the health, social, and family background information that is made known to the agency.** Agencies should clearly state in writing to prospective adoptive parents that the agency can disclose only known health and other background information; that is, information that has been provided to the agency prior to placement. Agencies should state specifically that they undertake no independent investigation either to obtain health and other background information or to verify the accuracy of information that is received. As in the birth parent medical questionnaire, written information on the child's health and other background information should include a statement that the agency makes no representations or warranties as to accuracy or completeness.

- **Any adopted child may have physical or mental health problems and/or developmental or behavioral issues, either diagnosed or undiagnosed.** Agencies should advise adoptive parents in writing that any child who is adopted may have physical, psychological, or developmental problems about which the agency has no information. Agencies should not state in their documents, as some agencies currently do, that all medical information will be disclosed to adoptive parents, with the exception of "undetected" or "undiagnosed" medical conditions. This type of representation does not take into consideration a number of situations, including the possibility of problems that are known to the birth family or the sending country but which are not communicated to the agency, and the possibility of conditions or diseases for which the child may be at risk because of genetic or prenatal factors unknown to the agency. Agencies more accurately and appropriately convey the scope of information being disclosed as all "information made available to the agency."

- **The agency cannot and, therefore, is not guaranteeing the present or future health or development of any child. It is critical that agencies clearly convey to prospective adoptive parents that the present and future health of a child cannot be guaranteed.** This information underscores for adoptive parents that a child may have problems about which the agency has no information or that a child may develop problems at a later date for which there are currently no indications. Although courts have recognized that agencies cannot and are not expected to guarantee a child's health and development, it is wise for agencies to expressly state that no guarantee is being made.

## Staff Training

A final area on which agencies should focus is staff training. Agencies should ensure that staff are thoroughly familiar with standards of quality practice in collecting and communicating health and other background information. Staff should have a clear understanding of the importance of such information for the child, the birth family, prospective adoptive parents, and the adoptive family. Staff also should have skills in working with birth families to obtain needed information and in fully and accurately conveying that information to prospective adoptive families. Staff should be familiar with and able to effectively use the agency's required documentation related to the gathering and disclosure of health and other background information.

Equally important in staff development is attention to the attitudes that staff may have about adoption in relation to gathering and sharing background information. A staff member's own perspectives, experiences, and biases may impact his or her own work in this area, and self-awareness and acknowledgment of personal views can greatly enhance practice. For example, at one agency, a staff member conducting initial information sessions for persons interested in international adoption regularly begins by encouraging prospective adoptive parents to recognize that adoption (like life itself) is full of risks. She openly identifies herself as being, personally, a risktaker and tells parents that international adoption has risks that she would readily take but that are not appropriate for everyone, including the potential that a child will experience developmental delays as a result of early institutionalization. Similarly, a social worker at another agency who speaks with prospective adoptive parents about children with Down's Syndrome regularly discloses that her own brother is affected by Down's Syndrome. Through sharing that information, she gives families an opportunity to talk to someone with personal experience and conveys to them that her own experience and outlook may be different from their own. Agencies can help staff develop the knowledge and skills they need in the area of information collection and disclosure by providing opportunities for staff to identify their personal views and experiences and integrate those aspects into their professional practice.

## A Final Issue: Liability and Insurance

In addition to many practice issues associated with potential liability for wrongful adoption, agencies also must consider whether their liability insurance policies offer sufficient coverage in the event of wrongful adoption claims. Agencies may assume that they have adequate protection in their general liability and umbrella insurance policies. These policies, however, are generally limited to claims of bodily personal injury and do not include coverage for the types of injury typically asserted in wrongful adoption suits. Agencies should have, in addition to general liability policies, professional liability coverage to cover claims related to professional practice as well as directors' and officers' liability insurance that includes coverage for claims concerning professional services.

With regard to the scope of the agency's professional liability coverage, there should be, at a minimum, coverage for negligence. Most professional liability policies will exclude coverage for intentional wrongdoing and for discriminatory conduct. Some insurance carriers, however, may agree to cover the defense costs for a fraud or discrimination claim even though they will not cover any damage award if the agency is ultimately found liable. Typically, insurance carriers that agree to cover defense costs will assign personal injury lawyers to defend wrongful adoption suits. Agencies should attempt to negotiate the right to designate their own counsel in order to ensure representation by an attorney with expertise in adoption law and practice.

Finally, agencies should be aware that professional liability insurance coverage may be affected by the passage of time. Many agencies' professional liability policies are occurrence based, and, as a result, the insurance policy that the agency currently holds will cover the agency only if the policy was also in effect at the time of the alleged failure to disclose. As agencies change policies and coverage over time, they may find that the policy they held at the time of the alleged misconduct (which may be many years ago) is no longer in effect. In these instances, agencies may find that professional liability coverage is not available unless they have purchased continued coverage at an additional cost. Agencies should carefully review their current professional liability policies and take whatever steps possible to maximize coverage in the event of a claim of wrongful adoption.

# *Conclusion*

The development of the tort of wrongful adoption and the enactment of state statutes requiring the disclosure of health and other background information to prospective adoptive parents have had an important impact on adoption practice. Although adoption professionals have long recognized the benefits of disclosure for all parties to an adoption, there have been a notable number of cases in which agencies have failed to disclose children's known health and other background information with resulting harm to adoptive families who were unprepared to meet the medical, emotional, and developmental needs of the children whom they adopted. Courts that have recognized the tort of wrongful adoption and held agencies liable for fraudulent and negligent conduct have clearly outlined the type of misconduct for which agencies will be held liable.

There remain, however, questions about the nature and scope of wrongful adoption liability, particularly in the area of international adoption, where lawsuits have only recently begun to be filed. Questions also remain related to such questions as the duty to obtain full information, the communication of unverified and interpretative information, the use of genetic testing as part of pre-adoption evaluations, and the duty to disclose updated information. In spite of the lack of clarity in a number of areas, agencies can implement a range of recommendations that will enhance their ability to implement quality practice in the area of disclosure of health and other background information and limit their exposure to liability for wrongful adoption.

# References

Barnett, E. D., & Miller, L. C. (1996). International adoption: The pediatrician's role. *Contemporary Pediatrics, 13*(8), 29-46.

Barth, R. P., & Berry, M. (1988). *Adoption and disruption: Rates, risks, and responses.* New York: Aldine DeGruyter.

Betsworth, D. G., Bouchard, T. J., Jr., & Cooper, C. R. (1994). Genetic and environmental influences on vocational interests assessed using adoptive and biological families and twins reared apart and together. *Journal of Vocational Behavior, 44*(3), 263-278.

Blair, D. M. (1992). Getting the whole truth and nothing but the truth: The limits of liability for wrongful adoption. *Notre Dame Law Review, 67,* 850-869.

Blair, D. M. (1997). Liability of adoption agencies and attorneys for misconduct in the disclosure of health-related information. In J. H. Hollinger (Ed.), *Adoption law and practice,* Vol. 2 (pp. 16-1 - 6-150). New York: Matthew Bender.

Bouchard, T. J., Jr., & McGue, M. K. (1990). Genetic and rearing environmental influences on adult personality: An analysis of adopted twins reared apart. *Journal of Personality, 58*(1), 263-292.

*Burr v. Board of County Commissioners,* 23 Ohio St. 3d 69, 491 N.E.2d 1101 (Ohio 1986).

Cadoret, R. J., Yates, W. R., Troughton, E., Woodworth, G., & Stewart, M. A. (1995). Genetic-environmental interaction in the genesis of aggressivity and conduct disorders. *Archives of General Psychiatry, 52*(11), 916-924.

Cady, E., & Cady, F. (1956). *How to adopt a child.* New York: Whiteside & William Morrow.

Carp, E. W. (1995). Adoption and disclosure of family information: A historical perspective. *Child Welfare, 74*(1), 217-239.

Child Welfare League of America. (1988, 1978, 1959, 1932). *Standards for adoption service*. Washington, DC: Author.

Cole, E. (1990). A history of the adoption of children with handicaps. In L. M. Glidden (Ed.), *Formed families: Adoption of children with handicaps* (pp. 51-58). New York: Haworth Press, Inc.

Cole, E. S., & Donley, K. S. (1990). History, values and placement policy issues in adoption. In D. Brodzinskyn & M. D. Schechter (Eds.), *The psychology of adoption* (pp. 273-294). New York: Oxford University Press.

Daly, K. J., & Sobol, M. P. (1997). Key issues in adoption legislation: A call for research. In H. E. Gross & M. B. Sussman (Eds.), *Families and adoption* (pp. 145-158). New York: The Haworth Press, Inc.

Diamond, R. (1997, November 20). Personal communication, Adoption Resource Center, Spence-Chapin Services to Families and Children. New York.

Donley, K. (1990, Fall). Genetics and environment. *Adoptalk*, 8-9.

Dukette, R. (1984). Values issues in present day adoption. *Child Welfare, 63*, 233-243.

Engeler, A. (1997, September). An adoption tragedy: Did this baby ever have a chance? *Redbook*, 138-160.

Feigelman, W., & Silverman, A. R. (1986). Adoptive parents, adoptees and the sealed record controversy. *Social Casework, 67*, 219-226.

*Ferenc v. World Child*, 977 F. Supp. 56, 1997 U.S. Dist. Lexis 14457 (Washington, DC 1997).

Freundlich, M. (in press). The case against preadoption genetic testing. *Child Welfare*.

Freundlich, M. (1997). The Americans with Disabilities Act: What adoption agencies need to know. *CWLA AdoptioNews, 2*(2), 4-7.

*Gibbs v. Ernst*, 538 Pa. 193, 647 A.2d 882 (Pa. 1994).

Gonyo, B., & Watson, K. W. (1988). Searching in adoption. *Public Welfare, 64*(1), 14-22.

Groze, V., Haines-Simeon, M., & McMillen, J. C. (1992). Families adopting children with or at risk of HIV Infection. *Child & Adolescent Social Work Journal, 9*, 409-426.

*Harper and Johnson v. Adoption Center of Washington.* C.A. 94-985 (D.C. Super. Ct. Oct. 1995)(order granting motions for summary judgment).

Hollinger, J. H. (1990 & Supp. 1996). Aftermath of adoption: legal and social consequences. In J.H. Hollinger (Ed.), *Adoption law and practice*, Vol. 2 (pp. 13-1–13-105). New York: Matthew Bender.

Howe, R. A. W. (1995). Defining the transracial adoption controversy. *Duke Journal of Gender Law and Policy, 2*, 131-156.

Hutchinson, D. (1943). *In quest of foster parents: A point of view on homefinding.* New York: Columbia University Press.

*Juman v. Louise Wise Services*, 159 Misc.2d 314, 608 N.Y.S.2d 612 (N.Y. Sup. Ct. 1994), aff'd 211 A.D.2d 446, 620 N.Y.S.2d 371 (1st Dept. 1995), and 174 Misc.2d 49, 603 N.Y.S.2d 483 (N.Y.Sup. Ct. 1997)

Kohstaat, B., & Johnson, A. M. (1954). Some suggestions for practice in infant adoptions. *Social Casework, 35*, 91-99.

Kopels, S. (1995, January). Wrongful adoption: Litigation and liability. *Families in Society: The Journal of Contemporary Human Services*, 20-28.

LeMay, S. K. (1989). The emergence of wrongful adoption as a cause of action. *Journal of Family Law, 27*, 475-490.

Lewis, J. (1992, December). Wrongful adoption: Agencies mislead prospective parents. *Trial*, 75-78.

Lii, J. H (1998, February 8). Lawsuit against hospital over an adopted boy's HIV is seen as a first. *New York Times*, 35.

Lockridge, F. (1947). *Adopting a child.* New York: Greenberg.

Lomboso, P. J., Pauls, D. L., & Leckman, J. F. (1994). Genetic mechanisms in childhood psychiatric disorders. *Journal of the American Academy of Child and Adolescent Psychiatry, 33*(7), 921-938.

Maley, A. (1987). Note: Wrongful adoption: Monetary damages as a superior remedy to annulment of adoptive parents victimized by adoption fraud. *Indiana Law Review, 20*, 709-744.

*Mallette v. Children's Friend and Service*, 661 A.2d 67 (R.I. 1995).

*Meracle v. Children's Service Society of Wisconsin*, 149 Wis.2d 19, 437 N.W.2d 532 (Wis. 1989).

Merkel-Holguin, L. (1996). *Children who lose their parents to HIV/AIDS: Agency guidelines for adoptive and kinship placement.* Washington, DC: Child Welfare League of America.

*M.H. and J.H.L. v. Caritas Family Services*, 475 N.W.2d 94 (Minn. Ct. App. 1991), rev'd in part, aff'd in part, 488 N.W.2d 282 (Minn. 1992).

*Michael J. v. Los Angeles County Department of Adoptions*, 201 Cal. App. 3d 859, 247 Cal. Rprt. 504 (1988).

*Mohr v. Massachusetts*, 421 Mass. 147, 653 N.E. 2d 1104 (Mass. 1995).

*Moreau v. Roman Catholic Diocese of New York*, No. 13057196 (N.Y. Sup. Ct. Filed September 6, 1996).

Mosher, W. D., & Bachrach, C. A. (1996). Understanding U.S. fertility: Continuity and change in the national survey of family growth, 1988-1995. *Family Planning Perspectives, 28* (1): 4-12.

National Adoption Information Clearinghouse. (1991). *Policy and practice issues for adoption and foster care of HIV-infected children.* Rockville, MD: Author.

Nelson, K. A. (1985). *On the frontier of adoption: A study of special needs adoptive families.* Washington, DC: Child Welfare League of America.

Newman, N. (1996). Bid to reform adoption laws isn't progress. *National Law Journal, 18*(24), A21.

*Nierengarten v. Lutheran Social Services of Wisconsin*, 209 Wis. 2d 538, 563 N.W.2d 181 (Wis. Ct. App. 1997).

Office of Civil Rights and Administration for Children and Families. (1997). *Memorandum: Interethnic Adoption Provisions of the Small Business Job Protection Act of 1996.* Washington, DC: U.S. Department of Health and Human Services, Office of the Secretary.

Oppenheim, E. (1997). Personal communication, Interstate Compact on Adoption and Medical Assistance, American Public Welfare Association. Washington, DC.

Raymond, L. (1955). *Adoption . . . and after*. New York: Harper and Row.

Rauch, J. B. & Rike, N. (no date). *Adoption worker's guide to genetic services*. Chelsea, MI: The National Resource Center for Special Needs Adoption.

Rice, T., Vogler, G. P., & Perusse, L. (1989). Cardiovascular risk factors in a French Canadian population: Resolution of genetic and familial environmental effects on blood pressure using twin, adoptees, and extensive information on environmental correlates. *Genetic Epidemiology, 6*(5), 571-588.

*Roe v. Catholic Charities of the Diocese of Springfield*, 225 Ill. App. 3d 519, 588 N.E.2d 354 (Ill. App. Ct. 1992).

Sachdev, P. (1989). *Unlocking the adoption files*. Lexington, MA: Lexington Books.

Schapiro, M. (1956). *A study of adoption practice* (Vol. 1). New York: Child Welfare League of America.

Seelye, K. (1997, November 2). Couple accused of beating daughters tell of adoption ordeal. *New York Times*, p. B37, B42.

Sullivan, A. (1998, January 30). Personal communication. Director of Adoption, Child Welfare League of America.

Watson, A. E. (1918). The illegitimate family. *Annals of the American Academy of Political and Social Science, 77*, 103-116.

Wertkin, R. A. (1986). Adoption workers' views on sealed records. *Public Welfare, 44*, 15-17.

# About the Authors

 Madelyn Freundlich is Executive Director of The Evan B. Donaldson Adoption Institute, New York, New York. She is a social worker and lawyer whose work has focused on child welfare policy and practice for the past decade. She formerly served as General Counsel for the Child Welfare League of America and as Associate Director of Program and Planning for the Massachusetts Society for the Prevention of Cruelty to Children. She is the author of a number of books and articles on child welfare law, policy, and financing. Her most recent writing has focused on the impact of welfare reform on foster care and special-needs adoption, interstate adoption law and practice, genetic testing in adoption evaluations, and confidentiality in adoption law and practice. Ms. Freundlich received her master's degrees in social work and public health, and she also holds a J.D. and LL.M.

 Lisa Peterson is Legal Consultant to Spence-Chapin Services to Families and Children, New York, New York. Spence-Chapin is a private, not-for-profit, state-licensed child placement agency and CWLA member that specializes in domestic, international, and special needs adoption. Ms. Peterson was formerly a corporate attorney with Paul, Weiss, Rifkind, Wharton & Garrison in New York City from 1986 to 1994. She has given presentations on the subject of wrongful adoption to the Joint Council on International Children's Services and the Association of Administrators of the Interstate Compact on Adoption and Medical Assistance.

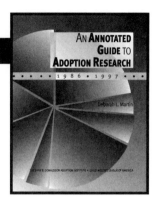

CHILD WELFARE LEAGUE OF AMERICA

# An Annotated Guide to Adoption Research: 1986–1997
## Deborah Martin

Published in conjunction with The Evan B. Donaldson Adoption Institute, the *Annotated Guide to Adoption Research* presents approximately 850 abstracts of qualitative and quantitative adoption research conducted and/or published between 1986 and 1997, encompassing clinical and nonclinical samples, case studies, longitudinal studies, epidemiological studies, grounded theory, experimental research, and single-subject research. A valuable resource for all members of the adoption community!

**Selected Contents:**

| | | |
|---|---|---|
| Adolescents | Intercountry Adoption | Search & Reunion |
| Adoptive Parenthood | Minnesota Transracial | Service Providers |
| Adulthood | Adoption Studies | Policies & Programs |
| Attachment | Open Adoption | Single Parent Adoption |
| Attitudes Toward Adoption | Open/Sealed Records | Special Needs Adoption |
| Birthparents | Orphanages & | Statistics & Trends |
| Childhood/Middle Years | Institutionalization | Author Index |
| Generic/Environment | Permanency Planning | |

To Order:   1998/0-87868-708-4   Stock #7084      $24.95

Write:  CWLA c/o PMDS          Call:  800/407-6273
        P.O. Box 2019                 301/617-7825
        Annapolis Junction, MD 20701
e-mail: cwla@pmds.com         Fax:   301/206-9789

Please specify stock #7084. Bulk discount policy (not for resale): 10-49 copies 10%, 50-99 copies 20%, 100 or more copies 40%. Canadian and foreign orders must be prepaid in U.S. funds. MasterCard/Visa accepted.

# NEW!!
## REVISED EDITION!

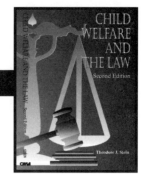

CHILD WELFARE LEAGUE OF AMERICA

## Child Welfare and the Law
### *Theodore J. Stein*

Throughout the 20th century, the law has shaped child welfare. Federal and state legislative actions affect the number of programs available to help children and their families, and cyclical preferences favoring certain services over others, as well as fluctuations in funding, condition the demand for social work staff and influence the knowledge and skills that are valued.

*Child Welfare and the Law* will enhance the reader's knowledge of the law and of the special relationship between the law and social work practice in child welfare. Author Theodore J. Stein, a professor of Social Welfare as well as an attorney, provides an overview of the child welfare and judicial systems, then examines the federal and state legislative and judicial foundations of modern child welfare practice; court decisions and their impact on the rights of biological parents, foster parents, and children; class action suits and their impact on child welfare; and the role of child welfare workers in the legal process. Appendices provide detailed instruction on conducting legal research and excerpts from a consent decree.

To Order:  1998/0-87868-728-9   Stock #7289          $34.95

Write:  CWLA c/o PMDS                 Call:  800/407-6273
        P.O. Box 2019                        301/617-7825
        Annapolis Junction, MD 20701
e-mail:  cwla@pmds.com                Fax:   301/206-9789

Please specify stock #7289. Bulk discount policy (not for resale): 10-49 copies 10%, 50-99 copies 20%, 100 or more copies 40%. Canadian and foreign orders must be prepaid in U.S. funds. MasterCard/Visa accepted.